LESSONS
with
LIAM

To my wife Jan, for her constant support and encouragement

ACKNOWLEDGEMENTS

To Russell Smith, for his professionalism and amazing eye for detail. For his beautiful photography and for making this such a fun book to work on.

To all of the people involved at Media24 Books, especially Daleen van der Merwe for having such vision and flair to make this book come together. To Melanie Kriel, for all of her hard work and for putting up with Russell and I changing our minds. To Joy Clack, for being so efficient and fast. To Patrick Collins, who put us all in touch.

To all of the team at Chefs Warehouse & Cookery School, Cape Town who always work above and beyond the call of duty: Peter Brophy, Leon Roelofse, Rose Vellem, Rachel Nicholson, and to John van Zyl who worked alongside me with all of the preparation for this book. Thank you all.

Human & Rousseau
An imprint of NB Publishers

First published in 2012 by Human & Rousseau
An imprint of NB Publishers
40 Heerengracht, Cape Town 8000

Commissioning Editor Daleen van der Merwe
Design Melanie Kriel
Editing and index Joy Clack (Bushbaby Editorial Services)
Proofreading Laetitia Sullivan (Bushbaby Editorial Services)
Photography Russell Smith

Reproduction by Resolution Colour Pty (Ltd), Cape Town
Printed and bound by Craft Print, Singapore

ISBN 978-0-7981-5729-2
EPUB 978-0-7981-5730-8

LESSONS with LIAM

LIAM TOMLIN:
A professional chef in your kitchen

Photography by RUSSELL SMITH

Human & Rousseau
An imprint of NB Publishers

INTRODUCTION

This is not just a book of recipes but rather covers a very small but important spectrum of basic cooking skills. A lot of cookery books take for granted that the reader will know how to tackle basic, ordinary tasks such as blanching vegetables, butchering meat or filleting fish. Even with the help of pictures some techniques – like boning a duck or filleting a whole salmon or cooking and preparing a live crab – will still be daunting and difficult to perform. These require patience and experience; only with time and much practice will they become easier.

Having spent most of my professional life in restaurant kitchens and now owning and operating two cookery schools, I have noticed that, when watching young chefs cook or teaching a group of people in the school, the biggest drawback to a good result in any kitchen is a lack of knowledge of very basic cooking techniques and an uncertainty about the handling and preparation of everyday ingredients.

I have come across many competent and keen cooks who are very creative with their cooking but are let down by the final dish because they don't have a grasp of the basics. Solid background is essential and must precede creativity and inventiveness. It is easy to serve a beautifully presented dish, but the dish will only be a real success if the fish is first cleaned and filleted properly, cooked perfectly, seasoned correctly and the sauce that it is being served with has been made from a good stock, reduced to the right consistency, finished with suitable flavours and seasoned correctly, and all served at the correct temperature. All of this requires practice, organisation, time and patience.

I often notice people preparing food and cooking for hours without once tasting the food. This is such an important part of the cooking process. It is vital to taste and keep tasting as you cook each stage of each dish. Over time you will train your palate to be able to add just the right amount of seasoning to your food and to understand at what stage of a dish to season it. The timing of when flavour is added will affect the food that is being cooked. Delicate herbs such as basil or chervil added during cooking will have a very different impact on a dish than when they are added at the end of cooking and still retain all of their flavour.

As an experienced chef I sometimes take for granted my ability to chop, slice, butcher and fillet with speed and accuracy, but that only came with time, training and practice. There are no real secrets or tricks in the professional kitchen, just techniques and knowledge that can only be acquired with prolonged effort, experience and commitment. Start with simple techniques and work gradually towards more involved and complicated skills that may have to be performed several times before being perfected. Only after time and practice will you begin to see and taste the results and benefits of your hard work. But it is certainly worth the effort.

LIAM TOMLIN

CONTENTS

NOTES ON RECIPES

There is a big difference between the professional and domestic kitchen. The professional kitchen is designed with self-contained sections for different food preparation tasks, each with its own work space, stovetops, ovens and refrigeration. Then there are the added luxuries such as plate warmers, hot lights, salamanders, slicing machines, blenders, electric mincers, mixing bowls, ice-cream machines and a selection of ovens set at different temperatures and modes to accommodate all manner of dishes. All this allows for a menu with a variety of dishes prepared in different ways, using different techniques and cooking methods. Following are simply a few guidelines to help with the recipes in this book.

- For more detailed information about the ingredients used in the recipes, read the introduction at the beginning of each chapter.
- Read through the list of ingredients and method before starting a recipe to enable you to calculate the time required to make the dish. Prepare the basic recipes first. If a recipe calls for a stock, make double the quantity and freeze one half for future use. If you apply this rule, you will soon build up a useful supply of basic ingredients such as stocks, flavoured oils, rendered duck fat, syrups and seasonings.
- Concentrate on the flavour of a dish and serving it at the correct temperature rather than trying to do fussy presentation and allowing elements of the dish to go cold.
- There are no weights or measurements given for seasoning such as salt, pepper or lemon juice. You should taste as you proceed. It is very difficult to 'bring back' a dish that has been over-salted or has had too much lemon juice added to it without diluting the flavour of the dish with stock or cream. So, season to taste.
- Where alcohol is called for, make sure it is reduced as per the recipe to remove the acidic taste that comes from unevaporated alcohol. When using wine in a dish, choose a wine that you would drink yourself. Treat it as an ingredient. It should be of good quality, just like your raw ingredients.
- Where a recipe calls for an ingredient to be blanched, such as vegetables or pasta, cook it in plenty of boiling salted water so that the temperature of the water is maintained when the ingredient is immersed in the water. Have a bowl of iced water ready to refresh the ingredient being blanched (to stop the cooking process and preserve the colour, texture and flavour). Some foods such as bacon are blanched to reduce their salt content. Others can be blanched in hot oil.
- In the preparation of vegetable stocks, the chicken stock can be replaced with water to render them suitable for vegetarian dishes.
- Always wash and dry vegetables before using, except for mushrooms and courgette flowers. These need only to be wiped with a damp cloth to remove any dirt that might be on or in them.
- Use only fresh herbs unless otherwise stated.
- Oven temperatures and cooking times may vary depending on the equipment being used.
- Use heavy-based stainless steel saucepans and cast-iron pans. These give much better results than cheaper pots and pans, which tend to wear out quickly, buckle and distribute uneven heat, resulting in inconsistently coloured and unevenly cooked ingredients. Stainless steel and cast-iron pans can be used to seal meats, fish and vegetables on the stovetop and can then be transferred straight into a hot oven so that the cooking temperature can be maintained at all times.
- When buying kitchen equipment, buy the best quality that you can afford, collecting pieces over a period of time. A well-considered, quality piece should last a lifetime.

SEASONING

Before seasoning food there are a few points to remember, the first being that to season and to flavour food are two different things. Seasoning includes salt being added to a preparation, while other seasonings such as thyme and citrus juice transfer flavour to food.

Salt brings out the moisture in food. It is used as the main ingredient in almost all foods cured, brined or preserved. Salt added to raw ingredients such as fish, meat and vegetables will draw the moisture from them, which is vital in the preparation of confit (*Basic Technique 12, page 168*) or to draw the juice from vegetables such as tomatoes or aubergines. However, it is not good for a delicate piece of fish or shellfish such as scallops, so these should be seasoned just before or during cooking.

If serving fish with the skin on, a little salt rubbed into the skin 15 minutes before cooking will draw moisture and result in a nice crisp skin but the flesh should be protected.

The flavour of some foods is enhanced by seasoning before the cooking process and other foods, such as deep-fried foods, are best enhanced by seasoning after the cooking process.

Liquid foods like stocks, soups and sauces are generally seasoned after cooking because the evaporation of water can make them more salty than intended, particularly if you are reducing them to concentrate their flavour. When reducing liquids such as stocks and sauces to concentrate their flavour, it is best to season them once reduced to prevent them becoming too salty.

Take into consideration the high salt content when using ingredients such as anchovy, pancetta, nam pla or soy sauce in a dish, and allow for this when seasoning.

My preference is for Maldon sea salt as it is a very delicate flake that can be easily ground down between your fingertips or with a pestle and mortar. It is also a good table salt.

When using citrus fruit or vinegars such as lemon juice or balsamic, add gradually and taste after each addition as once a dish is over-seasoned it is very difficult to rectify without diluting the original flavours. It is a lot easier to rectify a bland sauce, soup or dressing with a pinch of salt or sugar or a dash of vinegar or squeeze of lemon juice. Use freshly ground white pepper to avoid unsightly specks of black pepper in sauces.

Citrus is a great all-year round fruit with many different varieties popping in and out of season. It has endless uses, particularly for seasoning and flavouring different foods; from a simple squeeze of fresh juice, to a sauce such as a fish velouté, a hollandaise sauce or beurre blanc. By drying and grinding the zest to a powder and mixing it with Maldon sea salt it can be used as a sharp, tangy seasoning for fish and shellfish such as pan-fried scallops, red mullet and John Dory. It may also be used to season chicken, duck and guinea fowl. Citrus is commonly found in Asian cuisine, especially in Thai and Vietnamese dishes.

The zest can be used to infuse oils and vinaigrettes such as Lemon Oil (*Basic Recipe 27, page 68*), Lemon à la Grecque (*page 61*) and Escabèche (*page 92*), or when marinating meats to confit, or fish for soups and stews such as bouillabaisse.

When using flavoured oils such as truffle, sesame, walnut or hazelnut, use them sparingly and add them gradually and with respect as they are often very intense in flavour and can overpower a dish. Flavoured oils are not normally served neat, but rather are blended with other ingredients.

Most importantly, season to taste and keep tasting as you cook at each stage of each dish. Over time you will train your palette to be able to add just the right amount of seasoning to your food and understand at what stage of a dish to season it. The timing of when flavour is added will affect the food that is being cooked. Delicate herbs such as basil or chervil added at the end of cooking will still have all their flavour, but will lose much of it if added during cooking.

CONVERSION CHARTS

LIQUID MEASURES

Metric	Imperial	US
60 ml	2 fl oz	¼ cup
125 ml	4 fl oz	½ cup
250 ml	8 fl oz	1 cup
300 ml	10 fl oz / ½ pint	1¼ cups
625 ml	20 fl oz / 1 pint	2½ cups
1 litre	35 fl oz	1 quart / 4 cups

SMALL MEASURES

¼ tsp	1 ml
½ tsp	2.5 ml
1 tsp	5 ml
1 tbsp	15 ml

DRY MEASURES

25 g	1 oz
50 g	2 oz
100 g	4 oz
225 g	8 oz
500 g	1 lb 2 oz
900 g	2 lb
1.3 kg	3 lb

LENGTHS

5 mm	¼ inch
1 cm	½ inch
2.5 cm	1 inch
10 cm	4 inch
15 cm	6 inch
30 cm	12 inch

OVEN TEMPERATURES

Gas	°C	°F	Oven Temperature
¼	110	225	Very cool
1	140	275	Cool
3	160	325	Warm
4	180	350	Moderate
7	220	425	Hot
9	240	475	Very hot

STOCKS

In the past, stocks made from bones used to be cooked for 12–16 hours, or sometimes even for days, and the stockpot used to be a dumping ground for all types of waste and mistakes in the kitchen. But in order to produce good sauces or soups it is absolutely essential to have a stock that has been prepared carefully using the freshest ingredients available.

It is very time consuming to prepare a recipe if you still need to make the stock from scratch. When cooking at home it is good to have a ready supply of stocks and other basic ingredients to hand, which will enable you to work quickly and easily when making sauces, soups, braises and stews with great flavour. There are no real shortcuts if you want a really good stock. If you only have time to make one stock, I would suggest white chicken stock because it is simple and quick to make and the most versatile of all the stocks used in the professional kitchen.

Cooking times for different flavoured stocks vary from 20-minute fish stock to the more time-consuming veal stock. The most commonly used stocks are white chicken, brown veal, vegetable and fish stock. These stocks, when boiled down and without any additions, are used as flavourings for dishes such as risottos and braises. When a binding element is added, such as vegetables or compound butters, these stocks become basic soups and sauces from which many others are derived. When making stocks, always make a little extra and freeze them so that you will always have them to hand.

There are some basic rules to follow to achieve a full-flavoured stock. All stocks should begin with good-quality, fresh ingredients. Bones, vegetables, fresh herbs, spices and wine must be of the best quality available.

Choose bones that have a good covering of meat on them, as this will ensure a good depth of flavour to the finished stock. Bones should be chopped into small pieces to extract maximum flavour from them. Wash chicken and fish bones under cold running water until the water runs clear, to remove any trace of blood that could turn the stock cloudy or bitter.

Wash and peel all vegetables to be used in the stock, except for mushrooms – they just need a wipe with a damp cloth. Chop vegetables into small pieces to extract maximum flavour.

Barely cover the ingredients with cold water to achieve a more concentrated and intense flavour. Too much water will dilute the flavours, resulting in a weak, watery stock instead of a strong, gelatinous one. If necessary more cold water can be added during cooking.

Always start the stock using cold water. When covered with cold water, the blood and other impurities in the bones will dissolve, rising to the surface as the water heats. If covered with hot water, these impurities will coagulate and disperse throughout the stock, turning it cloudy. Skim off any impurities that float to the surface of the stock as it simmers. Allow stock to slowly come to the boil, and then simmer to allow the ingredients to impart all of their flavour.

As soon as a stock has come to the boil, reduce the heat to a simmer and continuously skim to remove any scum and impurities that rise to the surface. If not removed they will boil back into the stock and turn it cloudy. If the stock boils it will cause the solids to break down, also turning the stock cloudy.

Once the stock is refrigerated, any excess fat or impurities will rise to the surface and form a layer that can be easily scraped away.

Cooking a stock longer does not make it better or stronger in flavour. Long cooking can actually be detrimental, since the stock becomes heavy and loses its flavour. Follow the cooking times in the recipes precisely; only veal stock needs several hours' cooking.

If a brown stock is required, roast the bones and vegetables at 180 °C until golden brown, and then proceed with the recipe. (See Brown Chicken Stock, page 13 or Veal Stock, page 14.)

BASIC RECIPE 1

White Chicken Stock

Makes 2 litres

For other white-fleshed birds, such as quail or turkey, follow the same recipe and method. The addition of half a knuckle of veal when preparing this stock will make it extra rich and gelatinous. To make a white veal stock, replace the chicken with an equal weight of veal bones or trimmings, and then proceed as for White Chicken Stock, increasing the cooking time by 30 minutes.

2.5 kg raw chicken carcasses
3.5 L cold water
¼ bunch celery, roughly chopped
1 large leek, dark green leaves removed, roughly chopped
1 large onion, peeled and roughly chopped
150 g button mushrooms, sliced
½ head garlic, roughly chopped
2 sprigs fresh thyme
4 sprigs parsley
2 dried bay leaves
6 white peppercorns, crushed
salt

Remove any excess fat from the chicken carcasses. Chop the chicken bones into small pieces and wash under cold running water to remove any trace of blood. When the water runs clear, drain the bones in a colander.

Place the chicken bones in a large saucepan and cover with cold water. Bring to the boil, reduce the heat and simmer for 15 minutes, skimming frequently to remove the impurities that float to the surface.

Add the chopped vegetables, garlic, herbs, crushed white peppercorns and a large pinch of salt, and continue to cook for a further 45 minutes. Skim the stock frequently. Adjust the seasoning if necessary.

Pass the stock through a fine sieve into a stainless steel container, allow to cool and then refrigerate. Before using, remove any fat that has formed on the surface.

The chicken stock can be kept covered in the fridge for up to 3 days before using or up to 3 months in the freezer.

BASIC RECIPE 2

Double Chicken Stock

Makes 1 litre

A double stock is used to achieve a more concentrated flavour and deeper colour in sauces, soups, consommés and savoury jellies.

1 kg chicken wings
30 ml olive oil
1 stick celery, roughly chopped
1 small leek, dark green leaves removed, roughly chopped
½ large onion, roughly chopped
50 g button mushrooms, sliced
½ head garlic, peeled and roughly chopped
1.5 L chilled Chicken Stock (*Basic Recipe 1, see above*)

Chop the chicken wings into 4 pieces. Heat the olive oil in a heavy-based saucepan over a medium heat. Add half of the chopped chicken wings and sauté for 3–4 minutes without colouring.

Add the vegetables and garlic and continue to cook without colour for another 3 minutes.

Add the remaining raw wings and cover with the chilled chicken stock. Bring to the boil, reduce the heat and simmer for 30 minutes, skimming frequently to remove the impurities that float to the surface.

Add the herbs, crushed white peppercorns and a large pinch of salt and continue to cook for a further

2	sprigs fresh thyme
4	sprigs parsley
2	bay leaves
6	white peppercorns, crushed
	salt

30 minutes. Skim the stock frequently. Adjust the seasoning if necessary.

Pass the stock through a fine sieve into a stainless steel container, allow to cool and then refrigerate. Before using, remove any fat that has formed on the surface.

The double chicken stock can be kept covered in the fridge for up to 2 days before using or up to 3 months in the freezer.

BASIC RECIPE 3

Brown Chicken Stock

Makes 2 litres

This stock can be made with water but to achieve a richer flavour use a white chicken stock as the base liquid. For a more intense flavour and deeper colour use a base of half White Chicken Stock and half Veal Stock. Ensure both stocks are chilled when added to the browned bones to achieve a clear stock. The same method can be used for game bird carcasses, veal or lamb bones. Brown stocks are achieved by roasting the bones and deglazing (*déglaçage*) the pan with water, wine or stock to dislodge the caramelised sediment, which adds both colour and flavour to the stock. Brown stocks are richer, fuller-flavoured and more concentrated than white stocks.

2 kg	raw chicken carcasses or a mix of wings and necks, chopped into small pieces
75 ml	vegetable oil
3 L	cold water (or chilled White Chicken Stock or half White Chicken and half Veal Stock, *Basic Recipe 1 and 4, page 12 and page 14*)
2	onions, peeled and roughly chopped
2	carrots, peeled and roughly chopped
2	sticks celery, roughly chopped
250 g	button mushrooms, sliced
1	leek, white part only, roughly chopped
1	head garlic, halved
100 g	tomato paste

Preheat the oven to 180 °C.

Coat the bones in half of the oil and roast until browned, turning the bones frequently to ensure even colouring.

When the bones are roasted, drain and place in a heavy-based saucepan and cover with the cold water or stock. Bring to the boil, reduce the heat to a simmer and cook for 30 minutes, skimming frequently to remove all the impurities that float to the surface.

Pour the remaining oil into the same tray in which the bones were roasted, add the vegetables and garlic and roast for 20 minutes until caramelised.

Add a few dashes of water and stir the vegetables to loosen the sediment left from the bones. Mix the tomato paste through the vegetables and continue to roast for a further 10 minutes.

Add the vegetables to the stock. Continue to simmer the stock for a further 1–1½ hours, or until the stock has reduced by two-thirds. Skim the stock frequently. Pass the stock through a coarse sieve to remove the bones and vegetables.

Pass the stock through a fine sieve into a stainless steel container, allow to cool and then refrigerate.

Before using, remove any fat that has formed on the surface.

The brown chicken stock can be kept covered in the fridge for up to 3 days before using or up to 3 months in the freezer.

BASIC RECIPE 4

Veal Stock

Makes 2.5 litres

Broths and stocks are both made in a similar way. Using meat, bones, vegetables, seasonings and water, they are slowly simmered and transformed into flavoured liquids. Most stocks are made from bones, while broths are made mostly from meat. Stocks become richer from the gelatine released from the bones during cooking, while broths have a meatier flavour. Stocks are always strained to remove the solids; broths are normally served with the solid ingredients such as meat and vegetables that flavoured them. Stocks are too bland to be served on their own, but when reduced to concentrate their flavour and with the addition of other ingredients and thickening agents, such as cream and butter, they can be turned into sauces, soups or braised dishes.

Calves' hooves are added to stocks for the gelatine they release during cooking, which results in gelatinous, sticky stocks once passed through a sieve and chilled. Cut bones for stocks into small pieces, which will make them easier to roast and colour evenly and will also extract maximum flavour.

1	**calf's hoof, split**
6 kg	**fresh veal bones**
50 ml	**vegetable oil**
4 L	**cold water**
1	**onion, peeled and roughly chopped**
1	**carrot, peeled and roughly chopped**
1	**stick celery, roughly chopped**
100 g	**button mushrooms, sliced**
1	**small leek, white part only, roughly chopped**
½	**head garlic, roughly chopped**
75 g	**tomato paste**

Preheat the oven to 180 °C.

Coat the hoof and bones in half of the oil and roast until browned, turning the bones frequently to ensure even colouring.

When the bones are roasted, drain and place in a heavy-based saucepan and cover with the cold water. Bring to the boil, reduce the heat to a simmer and cook for 30 minutes, skimming frequently to remove all the impurities that float to the surface.

Pour the remaining oil into the same tray in which the bones were roasted, add the vegetables and garlic and roast for 20 minutes until caramelised.

Add a few dashes of water and stir the vegetables to loosen the sediment left from the bones. Mix the tomato paste through the vegetables and continue to roast for a further 10 minutes.

Add the vegetables to the stock. Continue to simmer the stock for a further 6 hours, or until the stock has reduced by two-thirds. Skim the stock frequently.

Pass the stock through a coarse sieve to remove the bones and vegetables. Pass the stock through a fine sieve into a stainless steel container, allow to cool and then refrigerate.

Before using, remove any fat that has formed on the surface.

The veal stock can be kept covered in the fridge for up to 4 days before using or up to 3 months in the freezer.

BASIC RECIPE 5

Game Stock

Makes 2.5 litres

Game stocks are made using the same method as veal stock, but the veal bones are replaced with game bones such as venison, hare or rabbit or game bird carcasses. Different herbs, spices and alcohol, such as juniper berries, orange rind and port, are used to enhance the game flavour.

6 kg	**fresh game bones and trimmings**
50 ml	**vegetable oil**
4 L	**cold water or chilled Chicken Stock (*Basic Recipe 1, page 12*)**
1	**onion, peeled and roughly chopped**
1	**carrot, peeled and roughly chopped**
1	**stick celery, roughly chopped**
100 g	**button mushrooms, sliced**
1	**small leek, white part only, roughly chopped**
½	**head garlic, halved**
100 ml	**red wine**
100 ml	**port**
75 g	**tomato paste**
250 g	**chopped tomato**
3	**juniper berries**
1	**sprig fresh thyme**

Preheat the oven to 180 °C.

Coat the bones and trimmings in half of the oil and roast until browned, turning the bones frequently to ensure even colouring.

When the bones are roasted, drain and place in a heavy-based saucepan and cover with the cold water or chicken stock. Bring to the boil, reduce the heat to a simmer and cook for 30 minutes, skimming frequently to remove all the impurities that float to the surface.

Pour the remaining oil into the same tray in which the bones were roasted, add the vegetables and garlic and roast for 20 minutes until caramelised.

Add the red wine and port and stir the vegetables to loosen the sediment left from the bones. Mix the tomato paste, chopped tomato and juniper berries through the vegetables and continue to roast for a further 10 minutes.

Add the vegetables to the stock. Continue to simmer the stock for a further 1–1½ hours, or until the stock has reduced by two-thirds. Add the sprig of thyme for the last 15 minutes of cooking. Skim the stock frequently. Pass the stock through a coarse sieve to remove the bones and vegetables.

Pass the stock through a fine sieve into a stainless steel container, allow to cool and then refrigerate.

Before using, remove any fat that has formed on the surface.

The game stock can be kept covered in the fridge for up to 3 days before using or up to 3 months in the freezer.

BASIC RECIPE 6

Fish Stock

Makes 1 litre

Fish stocks are normally white but can be made with different flavourings, such as tomatoes, saffron and red wine, depending on what the final stock will be used for.

2 kg	**fresh white fish bones, such as cod, John Dory or kingklip**
1	**medium onion, peeled and roughly chopped**
1	**small leek, white part only, roughly chopped**
1	**stick celery, roughly chopped**
1	**small bulb fennel, roughly chopped**
50 ml	**olive oil**
2	**cloves garlic, peeled and crushed**
100 ml	**Noilly Prat (dry vermouth)**
200 ml	**white wine**
2 L	**cold water**
12	**white peppercorns, crushed**
1	**bay leaf**
2	**sprigs fresh thyme**
2	**sprigs parsley**

Chop the fish bones into small pieces and wash under cold running water to remove any trace of blood. When the water runs clear, drain the bones in a colander.

Wash the chopped vegetables in cold water and drain.

Heat the olive oil in a heavy-based saucepan over a medium heat. Add the onion, leek, celery, fennel and garlic and sweat without colour for 5 minutes.

Add the fish bones and continue to sweat for a further 3 minutes without colour.

Add the Noilly Prat and white wine and cook until the alcohol has evaporated.

Pour the cold water over the bones and bring to the boil. Reduce the heat to a simmer and skim off any impurities that float to the surface.

When the stock is clear and the fish bones have sunk to the bottom of the saucepan, add the crushed peppercorns, bay leaf, thyme and parsley and continue to simmer the stock for a further 15 minutes.

Remove the stock from the heat and pass through a fine chinois into a clean saucepan. Discard the bones and vegetables.

Put the stock back onto the heat and reduce to 1 litre to concentrate the flavour.

Pass the stock through a fine sieve into a stainless steel container, allow to cool and then refrigerate.

Before using, remove any fat that has formed on the surface.

The fish stock can be kept covered in the fridge for up to 2 days before using or up to 3 months in the freezer.

2000
2 LITRES

BASIC RECIPE 7

Shellfish Stock

Makes 1.25 litres

This stock can be made with water, but to achieve a richer depth of flavour use Fish Stock as the base liquid. Ensure the fish stock is chilled when added to the browned shells to achieve a clear stock. Slow-roasting the shells and vegetables gives the stock a deeper colour and more intense flavour. Once the shells and vegetables have been roasted, the pan or roasting tray is deglazed by adding water or alcohol to the pan and scraping up all the sediment, which is added to the stock for added flavour and colour.

700 g	**lobster or prawn shells and heads**
50 ml	**olive oil**
2	**carrots, peeled and roughly chopped**
1	**small bulb fennel, roughly chopped**
1	**onion, peeled and roughly chopped**
1	**stick celery, roughly chopped**
1	**small leek, white part only, roughly chopped**
2	**cloves garlic, peeled and crushed**
15 ml	**tomato paste**
6	**plum tomatoes, seeded and roughly chopped**
	pinch saffron threads
	pinch cayenne pepper
2	**strips orange zest**
2	**star anise**
150 ml	**Noilly Prat (dry vermouth)**
50 ml	**Pernod**
25 ml	**brandy**
1.5 L	**cold water or chilled Fish Stock (*Basic Recipe 6, page 17*)**
	salt
	freshly ground pepper
3	**large sprigs fresh tarragon**
2	**large sprigs fresh basil**

Rinse the lobster or prawn shells and heads under cold running water and chop into small pieces.

Heat the olive oil in a heavy-based saucepan over a medium heat and add the shells. Reduce the heat and gently cook the shells until they take on a deep red colour.

Stir in the vegetables and garlic and continue to cook until softened and lightly coloured.

Add the tomato paste, chopped tomatoes, saffron threads and cayenne pepper, the orange zest and star anise and cook for 5 minutes, stirring to prevent it from sticking to the base of the pan.

Deglaze with Noilly Prat, Pernod and brandy, allowing the alcohol to evaporate.

Cover the shells with the water or fish stock and cook over a low heat for 30 minutes, skimming frequently. Skim off any impurities that float to the surface.

Pass the stock through a coarse sieve, pressing down on the shells with the back of a ladle to extract as much flavour as possible. Season to taste with salt, freshly ground pepper and cayenne pepper.

Pass the stock through a fine chinois. Allow the stock to cool, add the tarragon and basil and allow to infuse for 30 minutes.

When ready to use, pass the stock through a fine chinois and discard the herbs.

The shellfish stock can be kept covered in the fridge for up to 2 days before using or up to 3 months in the freezer.

BASIC RECIPE 8

Mushroom Stock

Makes 2 litres

When making vegetable stocks, use one specific vegetable rather than using mixed vegetables to achieve a more intense and individual flavour. Use this mushroom stock for making risotto, soup, consommé or sauces. Using Chicken Stock as the base liquid will give the finished mushroom stock a stronger and more concentrated flavour. For vegetarian dishes, use water as the base liquid. By sautéing the mushrooms first it will give the finished stock a rich colour.

2 kg	button mushrooms
6	large field mushrooms, gills removed
50 ml	vegetable oil
1	clove garlic, crushed
4	shallots, peeled and sliced
300 ml	Madeira wine
	salt
	freshly ground pepper
3 L	cold water or chilled Chicken Stock (*Basic Recipe 1, page 12*)
50 g	dried cep mushrooms
4	sprigs fresh thyme
6	sprigs flat-leaf parsley
6	sprigs fresh tarragon

Wipe the mushrooms clean with a damp cloth and finely slice them.

Heat the oil in a large cast-iron pan until smoking. Add the mushrooms, garlic and shallots and sauté until golden brown. If the pan is not large enough, sauté the mushrooms in two batches as it is important that the pan maintains the heat, otherwise the mushrooms will release their juice and end up boiling in it, losing colour and a lot of flavour.

When nicely browned, add the Madeira and continue to cook until it has reduced by three-quarters.

Remove the pan from the heat and season the mushrooms lightly with salt and freshly ground pepper.

Transfer the mushrooms to a heavy-based saucepan, cover with the water or chicken stock and bring to the boil. Reduce the heat to a simmer and skim any impurities that float to the surface.

Add the dried cep mushrooms and simmer for 40 minutes. Add the herbs and continue to cook for a further 5 minutes. Check the seasoning and adjust if necessary.

Pass the stock through a fine sieve, pressing down on the mushrooms to extract as much flavour and colour as possible. Adjust the seasoning if necessary. Pour the stock into a stainless steel container, allow to cool and then refrigerate.

Before using, remove any fat that has formed on the surface.

The mushroom stock can be kept covered in the fridge for up to 2 days before using or up to 3 months in the freezer.

BASIC RECIPE 9

Court-Bouillon

Makes 1 litre

Translated, it literally means 'short boil' and is a seasoned poaching liquor used in place of water for cooking sweetbreads, brains, certain vegetables, lobsters and langoustines or whole fish. A *nage* is a version of a court-bouillon in which the vegetables are cut neatly so that they can be presented as part of a finished dish. The court-bouillon can be re-used up to three times, but don't be tempted to use it as a stock for soups or sauces as it is too acidic.

1 L	cold water
250 ml	dry white wine
1	onion, peeled and chopped
1	carrot, peeled and sliced
1	large stick celery, sliced
4	button mushrooms, sliced
1	small bulb fennel, sliced
1	small leek, white part only, washed and sliced
2	cloves garlic, peeled and crushed
1	sprig fresh thyme
1	bay leaf
1	large sprig parsley
	pinch sea salt
10	white peppercorns, crushed

Place all of the ingredients in a heavy-based saucepan. Bring to the boil and skim any impurities that float to the surface. Reduce the heat and simmer for 30 minutes.

Pass the stock through a fine sieve into a stainless steel container, allow to cool and then refrigerate.

The court-bouillon can be kept covered in the fridge for up to 2 days before using or up to 3 months in the freezer.

STAUB

Onion and Cider Soup

Serves 4

To achieve both the colour and sweetness required from the onions for this soup, they must be cooked slowly over a low heat until all of the water from the onions has evaporated and the sugars are released to achieve beautifully caramelised onions. For a cream of onion soup, add 70 ml fresh cream to the finished onion soup and cook for a further 5 minutes. Adjust the seasoning if necessary.

40 g	**unsalted butter**
400 g	**brown onions, peeled and finely sliced**
2	**sprigs fresh thyme**
250 ml	**sweet cider**
650 ml	**Chicken Stock or Veal Stock (*Basic Recipe 1 or 4, page 12 or 14*)**
	salt
	freshly ground pepper
8	**thin slices baguette**
25 g	**Gruyère cheese, grated**

Heat a heavy-based saucepan over medium heat. Add the butter and allow to melt before adding the onions. Reduce the heat and cook the onions slowly until they are golden brown and caramelised.

Add the thyme sprigs and stir through the onions. Add the cider and continue to cook until it reduces to a syrup.

Add the chicken or veal stock and continue to cook over a low heat for 40 minutes, skimming the surface frequently. Season to taste with salt and pepper.

Preheat the grill. Toast the baguette slices on both sides under the grill. Sprinkle over the grated Gruyère and place under the grill until gratinated.

Remove the thyme sprigs from the soup and divide it between 4 warm soup bowls.

Garnish with toasted croûtons and serve.

Shellfish Bisque

Makes 2 litres

You can make this bisque using the shells from lobster heads, which are available from some fishmongers. Alternatively, use the same recipe but replace the lobster shells with prawn shells to make prawn bisque. The shells must be slow-roasted to achieve the maximum colour and flavour from them.

2 kg	**lobster heads and shells or prawn shells**
50 ml	**vegetable oil**
2	**carrots, peeled and chopped**
1	**onion, peeled and chopped**
2	**sticks celery, chopped**
4	**cloves garlic, peeled and chopped**
30 ml	**tomato paste**
	pinch saffron threads
	pinch cayenne pepper
1	**strip orange zest**
2	**star anise**
100 ml	**white wine**
50 ml	**brandy**
3 L	**cold water, Fish Stock or Shellfish Stock (*Basic Recipe 6 or 7, page 17 or 19*)**
1	**small bunch fresh tarragon, roughly chopped**
4	**sprigs fresh thyme**
1	**small bunch fresh basil, roughly chopped**
80 ml	**fresh cream**
150 g	**unsalted butter, diced**
	salt
	freshly ground white pepper
	squeeze of fresh orange juice

Clean the lobster heads and shells or prawn shells under cold running water and chop into small pieces.

Heat the vegetable oil in a heavy-based saucepan over medium heat and add the shells. Gently roast until they take on a deep red colour.

Stir in the vegetables and garlic and continue to cook until softened and lightly coloured.

Add the tomato paste, a pinch of both saffron threads and cayenne pepper, the orange zest and star anise and cook for 3 minutes, stirring to prevent it from sticking to the base of the pan.

Deglaze with wine and brandy, and allow the alcohol to evaporate.

Cover the shells with the water, fish stock or shellfish stock and cook over a low heat for 40 minutes, skimming frequently. Stir from time to time to prevent the shells from sticking and burning to the base of the saucepan.

Pass the shellfish bisque through a coarse sieve, pressing down on the shells with the back of a ladle to extract as much flavour as possible.

Place the tarragon, thyme and basil in a fine sieve and pass the soup over them. Return to a clean saucepan over a medium heat. Whisk in the cream and butter. Taste and adjust the seasoning with salt, freshly ground pepper, cayenne pepper, a squeeze of fresh orange juice and a dash of brandy if necessary.

Serve immediately.

Roast Tomato Soup

Serves 4

I often use this recipe to make Roast Tomato Vinaigrette (*Basic Recipe 34, page 73*) to serve drizzled over a vine-ripened tomato salad or poured over a simple roast chicken served with a crisp green salad. To make a roast tomato vinaigrette, simply follow the first stage of the recipe and pass through a coarse sieve. Adjust to taste with olive oil, balsamic vinegar and Worcestershire sauce and add some chopped basil.

120 ml	**olive oil**
1	**small red onion, peeled and roughly chopped**
2	**cloves garlic, peeled and thinly sliced**
1	**red chilli, split and seeded**
1.5 kg	**overripe vine-ripened tomatoes**
3	**sprigs fresh thyme**
	balsamic vinegar
	salt
	freshly ground pepper
25 g	**sun-dried tomatoes**
15 ml	**tomato paste**
1 L	**water or Chicken Stock (*Basic Recipe 1, page 12*)**
	Worcestershire sauce
1	**small bunch fresh basil, roughly chopped**

Preheat the oven to 180 °C.

Pour the olive oil into a roasting tray and add the onion, garlic, chilli, vine-ripened tomatoes and thyme. Drizzle with balsamic vinegar. Lightly season with salt and freshly ground pepper. Place in the oven and roast for 30 minutes, or until the tomato skins begin to blister and burst, releasing their juices.

Stir in the sun-dried tomatoes and tomato paste and continue to cook for a further 10 minutes.

Transfer the contents to a heavy-based saucepan and add the water or chicken stock. Bring to the boil, reduce the heat to a simmer and cook for 30 minutes. Remove the soup from the heat.

Add the Worcestershire sauce and balsamic vinegar to taste. Add the basil, cover the saucepan with clingfilm and allow the flavours to infuse for 1 hour.

Pass the soup through a fine chinois, pressing down on the tomatoes to extract as much flavour and colour as possible. Adjust the seasoning if necessary.

Serve the soup either hot or cold. Drizzle with a little extra virgin olive oil and garnish with basil leaves.

Picture on next page

Tomato and Basil Consommé

Serves 4

This is not a classic consommé, as the stock is neither cooked nor clarified. Once the tomatoes are blended, hung and passed, they develop into a crystal clear and intensely flavoured consommé. The tomatoes must be slightly overripe for them to release all of their juice to receive maximum yield from them. With the addition of gelatine the consommé can be turned into a jelly to use as the base for terrines. It can also be used as a stock for tomato risotto, as it reduces during cooking and gives an intense flavour to the finished dish.

2 kg	**overripe vine-ripened or plum tomatoes**
3	**shallots, peeled and sliced**
1	**clove garlic, peeled and crushed**
3	**sprigs fresh chervil, roughly chopped**
3	**sprigs fresh tarragon, roughly chopped**
1	**small bunch fresh basil, roughly chopped**
100 ml	**white wine**
25 ml	**chardonnay vinegar or white wine vinegar**
	pinch Maldon sea salt
	pinch sugar
	freshly ground pepper
80 g	**Tomato Concassée (*Basic Technique 13, page 177*)**
20	**fresh baby basil leaves**
20	**fresh tarragon leaves**
24	**slices black olive**

Core the tomatoes and chop roughly. Place in a bowl with the sliced shallots, garlic, roughly chopped herbs, white wine, vinegar, sea salt, sugar and a twist of freshly ground pepper. Mix the ingredients together and pulse briefly in small batches in a food processor (to break down and to release the juice from the tomatoes). Refrigerate for 4 hours to allow the flavours to infuse.

Transfer the contents of the bowl into a double layer of muslin cloth and tie it up as tightly as possible. Place in a sieve over a large bowl to catch all the juice released from the tomatoes.

Return to the fridge for 1–2 hours. Press gently from time to time to extract as much liquid as possible.

By now the tomatoes will have released all their juice and the sediment will have settled on the bottom of the bowl. Using coffee filter paper or a clean piece of muslin cloth, carefully decant the consommé into a clean bowl, taking care not to disturb the sediment. Discard the sediment and tomato pulp.

If serving hot, place the consommé in a saucepan and gently warm over a very low heat. Lightly season the tomato concassée with salt and freshly ground pepper and spoon into a soup bowl. Pour over the consommé and garnish with the picked basil and tarragon leaves and slices of olive. It may also be served cold.

ml
5000

Sweet Corn and Basil Soup

Makes 1 litre

This is a perfect example of how a simple, full-flavoured soup can be made from just two or three ingredients. It is crucial that you use fresh corn on the cob, as frozen or tinned corn doesn't have the same sweet flavour as fresh and the cobs are used for making a sweet corn stock as the base of the soup.

Barely cover the corn with stock to achieve a more concentrated and intense flavour. Too much water will only dilute the flavours, resulting in a weak and watery soup. If the soup is too thick it can be thinned out with more stock.

4	**fresh sweet corn on the cob**
50 g	**unsalted butter, diced**
100 g	**finely sliced onion**
2	**cloves garlic, peeled and crushed**
4	**sprigs fresh thyme**
	salt
2 L	**cold water**
100 ml	**fresh cream**
	freshly ground white pepper
1	**small bunch fresh basil with stalks, roughly chopped**

To make the sweet corn stock, peel and remove all the outer leaves, stalks and fibres from the cobs of corn. Remove the corn kernels from the cobs and set aside until ready to use. Cut the cobs into three pieces.

Melt half of the butter in a heavy-based saucepan over medium heat. Add half of the onion and half of the garlic and sweat for 5 minutes without colouring, until the onion is soft and translucent.

Add the cob pieces, 2 sprigs of thyme and a good pinch of salt and cook for a further 5 minutes without colouring.

Add the cold water and bring to the boil. Reduce the heat and simmer the stock for 20 minutes, skimming it frequently before passing it through a fine sieve. Discard the cobs, onion and garlic.

Melt the remaining butter in a heavy-based saucepan over medium heat. Add the remaining onion, garlic and thyme and sweat for 5 minutes without colouring, until the onion is soft and translucent.

Add the corn kernels and a good pinch of salt and cook for a further 5 minutes without colouring.

Add the sweet corn stock and simmer for 20–25 minutes, skimming regularly. Continue to cook until the corn kernels are tender.

Add the cream and reduce the heat to a simmer. Cook for a further 5 minutes.

Remove the soup from the heat and ladle into a liquidiser in batches. Blend to a smooth purée. Pour the blended soup into a clean stainless steel bowl and allow to go cold before adding the basil. Adjust the seasoning if necessary.

Allow the basil to infuse for 1 hour or overnight before passing the soup through a fine sieve, pressing hard with the back of a ladle to extract as much flavour from the corn and basil as possible. Adjust the seasoning if necessary.

The soup can be served either hot or cold and garnished simply with baby basil leaves. The sweet corn soup will keep for up to 3 days in a sealed container in the fridge. Due to the high fat content from the cream, it does not freeze well.

Vichyssoise

Serves 4

Vichyssoise or leek and potato soup is a classic French soup made with a purée of leeks and potatoes and finished with cream and sliced chives. Normally it is served cold but is just as good served hot. It is a perfect first course to any meal and can be served in an espresso cup or shot glasses as an elegant canapé.

25 g	**unsalted butter**
1	**large potato (175 g), peeled and diced**
1	**large onion (150 g), finely sliced**
3	**small leeks, white part only (300 g), finely sliced**
25 ml	**Noilly Prat (dry vermouth)**
750 ml	**cold water or Chicken Stock (*Basic Recipe 1, page 12*)**
125 ml	**fresh cream**
	salt
	freshly ground pepper
50 ml	**extra fresh cream, whipped to ribbon stage**
1	**small bunch chives, snipped**

Melt the butter in a heavy-based pan over medium heat until foaming. Add the potatoes, onion and leeks and sweat without colour for 8–10 minutes.

Add the Noilly Prat and continue to cook until the alcohol has evaporated.

Pour in the water or chicken stock and bring to the boil. Reduce the heat and simmer for 20 minutes until the potato pieces are tender.

Add the cream and bring the soup back to the boil. Reduce the heat and simmer for a further 5 minutes. Lightly season to taste with salt and freshly ground pepper.

Pour the soup into a food processor and blend until smooth. Pass through a fine sieve into a clean stainless steel container. Press down hard on the vegetables to extract as much flavour as possible.

Pour the vichyssoise into 4 soup cups and spoon 5 ml of whipped cream on top. Garnish with the snipped chives.

Vichyssoise of Oysters

Serves 4

1	**quantity Vichyssoise (*see above*)**
12	**unshucked oysters**
	salt
	freshly ground pepper
8	**Oyster Beignets (*page 102*)**
50 ml	**extra fresh cream, whipped to ribbon stage**
1	**small bunch chives, snipped**

Prepare the vichyssoise as described in the recipe above.

Shuck the oysters and remove from the shells (*Basic Technique 4, page 100*). Reserve the oysters and their juice.

Add the oyster juice and 6 oysters in stages to the vichyssoise and blend with a hand-held blender. Taste from time to time to check whether less or more oysters and juice are required than is suggested in the recipe. After blending the oysters, taste the vichyssoise and adjust the seasoning if necessary.

Pass the vichyssoise through a fine sieve into a clean saucepan. Heat the vichyssoise until warm.

Pour the vichyssoise into 4 warmed soup cups and spoon 5 ml of whipped cream on top. Garnish with the snipped chives. Serve with 2 deep-fried oysters per portion.

Quail Consommé

Serves 4

It is possible to transform any intensely flavoured double stock or strong broth into a clear consommé by clarifying it with a raft. Clarifying is the process of removing particles from a stock by cooking it over a low heat with the addition of egg whites, minced meat, poultry or fish with vegetables (the raft), until the raft floats to the top to form a crust. This brings all the solids and impurities to the surface, leaving a crystal clear stock under the crust. (When preparing meat or fish for a consommé, as much fat as possible should be trimmed off before mincing it.)

Once the raft sets on the surface, a small hole is pierced through it to allow the steam to escape. The consommé is then gently simmered for 20–30 minutes until the raft is cooked and has released its flavour. It is very important that the consommé does not boil or the raft will break up and the consommé will become cloudy. When ready, the consommé is gently ladled out without disturbing the raft.

If not using consommé immediately, divide it into 250 ml batches and freeze. If using from frozen, defrost in the fridge overnight or tip the frozen block of stock into a saucepan and heat gently over a low heat. This minimises the risk of harmful bacteria forming. Consommé will keep for 3 months in the freezer.

150 g	**quail trimmings from breast or leg, trimmed of skin, fat and sinew, minced, or chicken mince**
1	**shallot, peeled and thinly sliced**
10 g	**julienne of leek**
10 g	**julienne of celeriac**
10 g	**julienne of carrot**
1	**clove garlic, peeled and thinly sliced**
2	**sprigs fresh thyme**
5	**fresh free-range egg whites**
	salt
	freshly ground pepper
2.5 L	**cold quail stock (see *Basic Recipe 1, page 12*)**

Place the quail or chicken mince in a bowl along with the shallot, leek, celeriac, carrot, garlic, thyme and the egg whites and beat them all together. Season lightly with salt and freshly ground pepper.

Pour the cold quail stock into a heavy-based saucepan and beat in the quail mince mixture so that it is evenly dispersed through the stock. Place the saucepan over a low heat and simmer gently, stirring frequently to prevent the solids from sticking to the bottom or around the sides of the saucepan.

After 30–35 minutes, the mince, egg whites and vegetables will coagulate and float to the surface, bringing all the impurities in the stock with them and forming a crust (raft). Once the raft has set on the surface, pierce a small hole through it with a tablespoon to allow the steam to escape. Continue to simmer gently for a further 20 minutes.

Remove the consommé from the stove and ladle it through a fine chinois lined with muslin cloth or coffee filter paper, taking care not to break the raft. Once the consommé has been passed, discard the raft. Taste and adjust the seasoning.

Serve immediately or allow to cool in the fridge until ready to use.

The consommé will keep in a sealed container in the fridge for 3 days or up to 3 months in the freezer.

To serve, reheat the consommé in a saucepan over a gentle heat, making sure that the consommé does not boil. Pour the consommé into warm bowls and serve with Larb of Quail (*page 36*).

VARIATIONS OF CONSOMMÉ

Lobster Consommé: Made exactly the same way as Quail Consommé, except the quail mince is replaced with minced white fish trimmings. Use the Shellfish Stock (*Basic Recipe 7, page 19*) instead of quail stock and add fennel to the raft.

Mushroom Consommé: Replace the minced quail with skinless minced chicken and add dried cep mushrooms and fresh tarragon to the raft. Clarify Mushroom Stock (*Basic Recipe 8, page 20*) and finish with a dash of sherry or Madeira wine. Add small morel mushrooms and sliced truffle just before serving.

Chicken Consommé: Made exactly the same way as Quail Consommé, but the minced quail is replaced with skinless minced chicken and Double Chicken Stock (*Basic Recipe 2, page 12*).

Larb of Quail

Serves 4

The larb can be made with minced pork, beef, chicken, quail or venison. The salad should be hot, salty and sour so add more lime or fish sauce to taste. Serve as an entrée or an accompaniment to Quail Consommé. If serving as a main course, serve it with a bowl of steamed rice and steamed Asian greens such as bok choy or tat soi on the side.

20 g	**raw basmati rice**
600 g	**minced quail, with all skin, bone and sinew removed**
	salt
	freshly ground pepper
	sugar
30 ml	**Thai fish sauce**
2	**small red chillies, seeded and finely sliced**
90 ml	**fresh lime juice**
4	**shallots, peeled and finely sliced**
2	**spring onions, finely sliced**
1	**small bunch fresh mint**
1	**small bunch fresh Thai basil**
1	**small cucumber, seeded and finely grated**
2	**heads iceberg lettuce**
1	**small bunch fresh coriander**

Put the rice in a dry frying pan and toast it over a low heat for 3–4 minutes, tossing it continuously until it becomes an even, golden brown colour all over.

Transfer the rice to a tray and allow to go cold. Grind the rice in a spice grinder to a fine powder. Set aside until ready to use.

Fry the quail mince with a pinch each of salt, pepper and sugar in a dry, non-stick frying pan for 1½–2 minutes, until just cooked but still slightly pink. Transfer the fried quail to a stainless steel bowl.

Stir in the fish sauce, sliced chillies and lime juice to taste. Mix in the rice, shallots, spring onions, mint, Thai basil and cucumber. Adjust the seasoning if necessary.

Remove the stalks from the iceberg lettuce and carefully peel the leaves off one by one, keeping them whole. Place an iceberg leaf in the centre of each serving plate and fill with the larb. Garnish with sprigs of coriander.

SAUCES AND COMPOUND BUTTERS

BASIC RECIPE 10

Clarified Butter

Makes 250–300 ml

Butter is made up of butterfat, milk solids and water. Clarified butter is the translucent golden-yellow butterfat left over after the milk solids and water are separated and removed. Whole, unsalted butter is heated over a low heat until it melts and the milk solids have sunk to the bottom of the pan. The clear yellow liquid that lies on top is clarified butter.

Clarified butter is used in making butter-based sauces such as Hollandaise (Basic Recipe 21, page 49) and béarnaise. The water in whole butter would break down the emulsion, whereas clarified butter, with the water removed, eliminates this problem.

Clarified butter is essential for sautéing as it doesn't burn as easily as whole butter and can be heated to higher temperatures. Clarified butter also doesn't spoil as easily as whole butter and can be refrigerated for several months.

500 g unsalted butter

Place the butter in a heavy-based saucepan over low heat. The milk solids will separate from the butter and a foam will form on the surface. Skim the foam from the surface of the melted butter, leaving a clear, golden clarified butter underneath.

Once all of the foam has been removed, carefully pour the butter into a clean, non-reactive container, leaving the milk solids behind. Refrigerate until it solidifies. Lift out the butter, leaving any excess milky sediment behind.

Reduced Veal Stock
(Veal Jus and Variations)

Makes 750 ml

Stocks consist mostly of water containing suspended flavourful particles. To thicken them, you can either reduce the amount of water or increase the amount of solids. Reducing stock is done by boiling the liquid until the solid particles suspended in it concentrate and reduce to the required consistency and thicken the resulting sauce. Since the solid particles are also the flavourful elements in the liquid, this technique, called reduction, creates intensely flavoured sauces.

To make any good sauce, it is vital that you have a good base. A well-flavoured stock is the true foundation of a sauce, especially in French cuisine.

It is vital to get the proportions of strong-flavoured ingredients precisely right, such as pungent spices, citrus fruit, pre-salted ingredients, herbs, vinegars and alcohol. These should be added in moderation and added gradually to taste.

Where alcohol is called for in a recipe, make sure it is reduced as instructed to remove the acidic taste that comes from unevaporated alcohol. When using wine, choose a wine that you would drink yourself. Treat alcohol as an ingredient. It should be of good quality, just like your raw ingredients.

BASIC RECIPE 11

Reduced Veal Stock (Veal Jus)

Makes 1.5 Litres

30 ml	**vegetable oil**
500 g	**beef trimmings, diced**
3	**shallots, peeled and sliced**
100 g	**button mushroom, sliced**
5 L	**Veal Stock (*Basic Recipe 4, page 14*)**
1	**sprig fresh thyme**
	salt
	freshly ground pepper
50 g	**chilled butter, diced**

Heat 25 ml vegetable oil in a heavy-based frying pan. Add the beef trimmings and cook over a medium heat until evenly browned. Drain the beef trimmings in a colander.

Return the pan to the heat and add the remaining oil to it. Add the shallots and mushrooms and sauté until golden brown, and then drain in the same colander with the beef trimmings.

When drained, place the beef trimmings, mushrooms, shallots, veal stock and thyme into a heavy-based saucepan and bring to the boil. Reduce the heat to a simmer and cook for 1½ hours, skimming the surface frequently to remove any impurities that float to the surface.

Pass the sauce through a sieve lined with a double layer of muslin cloth into a clean saucepan. Reduce to 1.5 litres over medium heat. Skim the surface frequently, season to taste with salt and freshly ground pepper and pass the sauce through the muslin cloth one last time.

Transfer to a clean container and refrigerate until ready to use.

Just before serving, reheat over medium heat and finish by whisking in the chilled butter, piece by piece, until completely incorporated into the sauce. Adjust the seasoning if necessary.

Variations of Reduced Veal Stock

BASIC RECIPE 12

Red Wine Jus

Makes 500 ml

10 ml	vegetable oil
3	shallots, peeled and sliced
1	clove garlic, sliced
	salt
750 ml	red wine
325 ml	port
1	sprig fresh thyme
500 ml	Veal Jus (*Basic Recipe 11, page 41*)
	freshly ground pepper
20 g	chilled butter, diced

Heat the oil in a heavy-based saucepan over medium heat. Add the shallots, garlic and a pinch of salt and sauté without colour until the shallots have softened.

Pour in the red wine and port, and add the thyme. Cook over medium heat until reduced by three-quarters.

Pass the reduction through a fine sieve.

In a separate saucepan, bring the veal stock to the boil. Add the red wine reduction to taste. The sauce will have a very deep, rich colour. Season to taste with salt and freshly ground pepper before passing through a sieve lined with a double layer of muslin cloth.

Just before serving, reheat over medium heat and finish by whisking in the chilled butter, piece by piece, until completely incorporated into the sauce. Adjust the seasoning if necessary.

BASIC RECIPE 13

Port Wine Jus

Makes 500 ml

10 ml	vegetable oil
3	shallots, peeled and sliced
1	clove garlic, sliced
	salt
750 ml	port
325 ml	red wine
1	sprig fresh thyme
500 ml	Veal Jus (*Basic Recipe 11, page 41*)
	freshly ground pepper
20 g	chilled butter, diced

Heat the oil in a heavy-based saucepan over medium heat. Add the shallots, garlic and a pinch of salt and sauté without colour until the shallots have softened.

Pour in the port and red wine, and add the thyme. Cook over medium heat until reduced by three-quarters.

Pass the reduction through a fine sieve.

In a separate saucepan, bring the veal stock to the boil. Add the port reduction to taste. The sauce will have a very deep, rich colour. Season to taste with salt and freshly ground pepper before passing through a sieve lined with a double layer of muslin cloth.

Just before serving, reheat over medium heat and finish by whisking in the chilled butter, piece by piece, until completely incorporated into the sauce. Adjust the seasoning if necessary.

BASIC RECIPE 14

Charcuterie Sauce

Makes 300 ml

This sauce makes the perfect match for roast pork, veal, beef and offal. To marinate the mustard seeds, place 25 g each brown and yellow mustard seeds in a bowl with 2 sprigs of tarragon and 1 sprig of thyme. Bring 150 ml water to the boil with 25 ml white wine vinegar, 2.5 ml sugar, a pinch of salt and freshly ground pepper. Pour the boiling liquid over the mustard seeds and allow to cool before placing them in the fridge for 12 hours to marinate and soften. They can be stored for up to a week before using.

If making pork jus, follow the recipe for Veal Stock (*Basic Recipe 4, page 14*) but replace the veal bones with pork bones and reduce as described in *Basic Recipe 11, page 41*.

250 ml	**Veal Jus (*Basic Recipe 11, page 41*)**
2	**vine-ripened tomatoes, blanched and diced**
5 ml	**capers, rinsed under cold running water**
4	**small gherkins, thinly sliced**
6	**baby pickled onions, quartered**
15 ml	**finely sliced flat-leaf parsley**
30 ml	**marinated mustard seeds (see note above)**
	salt
	freshly ground pepper

Bring the veal jus to the boil, reduce the heat and add all of the remaining ingredients. Gently warm through. Season to taste with salt and freshly ground pepper.

BASIC RECIPE 15

Balsamic Jus

Makes 500 ml

5 ml	**vegetable oil**
3	**shallots, peeled and sliced**
1	**clove garlic, sliced**
	salt
250 ml	**port**
50 ml	**aged balsamic vinegar**
350 ml	**Veal Jus (*Basic Recipe 11, page 41*)**
	freshly ground pepper
10 g	**chilled butter, diced**

Heat the oil in a heavy-based saucepan over medium heat. Add the shallots, garlic and a pinch of salt and sauté without colour until the shallots have softened.

Pour in the port and 20 ml balsamic vinegar. Cook over medium heat until reduced by three-quarters.

Pass the reduction through a fine sieve.

In a separate saucepan, bring the veal jus to the boil and add the balsamic reduction. Season to taste with salt and freshly ground pepper before passing through a sieve lined with a double layer of muslin cloth into a clean saucepan. Add the remaining balsamic vinegar to taste.

Just before serving, reheat over medium heat and finish by whisking in the chilled butter, piece by piece, until completely incorporated into the sauce. Adjust the seasoning if necessary.

BASIC RECIPE 16

Bordelaise Sauce

Makes 500 ml

5 ml	vegetable oil
3	shallots, peeled and sliced
1	clove garlic, sliced
	salt
250 ml	red wine
2	sprigs fresh thyme
1	small dried bay leaf
6	black peppercorns, crushed
350 ml	Veal Jus (*Basic Recipe 11, page 41*)
	freshly ground pepper
10 g	chilled butter, diced
50 g	bone marrow (soaked in cold water for 5 minutes)

Heat the oil in a heavy-based saucepan over medium heat. Add the shallots, garlic and a pinch of salt and sauté without colour until the shallots have softened.

Pour in the red wine. Add the thyme, bay leaf and crushed black peppercorns. Cook over medium heat until reduced by three-quarters.

Pass the reduction through a fine sieve.

In a separate saucepan, bring the veal stock to the boil. Add the wine reduction. Season to taste with salt and freshly ground pepper before passing through a sieve lined with a double layer of muslin cloth into a clean saucepan.

Just before serving, reheat over medium heat and finish by whisking in the chilled butter, piece by piece, until completely incorporated into the sauce. Adjust the seasoning if necessary.

Add the bone marrow and gently warm over a low heat for 1 minute. Do not boil the sauce or warm for too long as the bone marrow will melt and make the sauce very greasy.

BASIC RECIPE 17

Sauce Périgeux

Makes 250 ml

20 ml	truffle juice
20 ml	port
20 ml	Madeira wine
400 ml	Veal Jus (*Basic Recipe 11, page 41*)
10 g	chopped truffle
40 g	unsalted butter, chilled and diced
	salt
	freshly ground pepper

In a heavy-based saucepan over medium heat, reduce the truffle juice, port and Madeira to a syrup.

Add the veal jus and bring to the boil. Reduce the heat to low and continue to reduce the sauce until it coats the back of a spoon.

Add the chopped truffle and whisk in the butter, piece by piece, until fully incorporated into the sauce. Season to taste with salt and freshly ground pepper.

COMMON PROBLEMS WHEN MAKING SAUCES

- The sauce is bland as a result of not being reduced enough to concentrate flavour.
- The sauce is bland because it lacks seasoning.
- The sauce is too thick and needs to be diluted with more stock or water.

BASIC RECIPE 18

Sparkling Shiraz Jus

Makes 750 ml

10 ml	**vegetable oil**
3	**shallots, peeled and sliced**
1	**clove garlic, sliced**
750 ml	**sparkling shiraz**
325 ml	**port**
1	**sprig fresh thyme**
500 ml	**Veal Jus (*Basic Recipe 11, page 41*)**
	salt
	freshly ground pepper

Heat the oil in a heavy-based saucepan over medium heat. Add the shallots, garlic and a pinch of salt and sauté without colour until the shallots have softened.

Pour in 700 ml sparkling shiraz and the port, and add the thyme. Cook over medium heat until reduced by three-quarters.

Pass the reduction through a fine sieve.

In a separate saucepan, bring the veal jus to the boil and add the sparkling shiraz reduction. The sauce will have a very deep, rich colour. Season to taste with salt and freshly ground pepper before passing the sparkling shiraz jus through a sieve lined with a double layer of muslin cloth into a clean saucepan.

Add the remaining 50 ml sparkling shiraz just before serving.

BASIC RECIPE 19

Cep Cream Sauce

Makes 350 ml

For this and the Morel Cream Sauce (*Basic Recipe 20, page 47*), Veal Jus is reduced with port, Madeira and dried mushrooms to remove water and concentrate flavour. Cream is added and boiled until the water content of the cream evaporates and the proteins in the cream coagulate, causing it to thicken. Both of these sauces are perfect with veal, chicken or any dish with a sautéed mushroom garnish. A little of either sauce poured into a mushroom risotto just before serving will give it an added depth of flavour.

175 g	**dried cep mushrooms**
50 ml	**port**
50 ml	**Madeira wine**
150 ml	**Veal Jus (*Basic Recipe 11, page 41*)**
375 ml	**fresh cream**
	salt
	freshly ground pepper

Soak the ceps in the port and Madeira for 4 hours.

Place the mushrooms, port and Madeira in a heavy-based saucepan and bring to the boil. Lower the heat and reduce the alcohol by three-quarters.

Add the veal jus and reduce by half.

Pour in the cream and continue to cook until the sauce coats the back of a spoon. Season to taste with salt and freshly ground pepper.

Remove from the heat and allow the sauce to stand for at least 1 hour to allow the dried ceps to release their flavour into the sauce.

Pass the cep cream sauce through a fine chinois, pressing down on the ceps to extract as much flavour and colour as possible. Save the cep pulp, chop finely and add it to Mushroom Duxelle (*Basic Technique 19, page 186*).

Picture on next page

BASIC RECIPE 20

Morel Cream Sauce

Makes 350 ml

175 g	dried morel mushrooms
50 ml	port
50 ml	Madeira wine
150 ml	Veal Jus (*Basic Recipe 11, page 41*)
375 ml	fresh cream
	salt
	freshly ground pepper

Soak the morels in the port and Madeira for 4 hours.

Place the mushrooms, port and Madeira in a heavy-based saucepan and bring to the boil. Lower the heat to medium and reduce the alcohol by three-quarters.

Add the veal jus and reduce by half.

Pour in the cream and continue to cook until the sauce coats the back of a spoon. Season to taste with salt and freshly ground pepper.

Remove from the heat and allow the sauce to stand for at least 1 hour to allow the dried morels to release all their flavour into the sauce.

Pass the morel cream sauce through a fine chinois, pressing down on the morels to extract as much flavour and colour as possible. Save the morel pulp, chop finely and add it to Mushroom Duxelle (*Basic Technique 19, page 186*).

COMMON PROBLEMS WHEN MAKING CREAM SAUCE

- The cream used in the sauce is too old and separates when heated.
- Too much acidity in the sauce, such as too much lemon juice, overpowers the intended flavour of the sauce.
- The sauce is too thin because the cream has not been reduced enough.
- The sauce is too thick because it has been reduced too much. Dilute with a little stock or water.

Hollandaise Sauce and Variations

Emulsions are made from two liquids that don't naturally combine and can be either hot or cold depending on the fat used in the sauce. Egg yolks are used to stabilise emulsified sauces.

Mayonnaise is a cold emulsion sauce that emulsifies lemon juice, vinegar and water with oil. To make a warm emulsion sauce, such as hollandaise, the oil is replaced with Clarified Butter and the sauce is kept warm to keep the butter in a liquid state. For both sauces the emulsifier is the lecithin and lipoproteins in egg yolks. To make hollandaise, a higher proportion of yolks must be used because heating the yolks coagulates their protein, making them less able to coat the fat and hold them in suspension. The oil or butter must be added slowly with continuous whisking to break the fat into small droplets. Too much fat added too quickly will cause the sauce to separate as the emulsifier will not be able to coat all of the droplets of fat and prevent it from the appropriate connection with the water to form an emulsion. For cold emulsions it is important that all the ingredients are at room temperature. When making hollandaise, add a little lemon juice before adding the butter as the acid raises the yolks' coagulation point, making it less likely to curdle.

Traditional sabayon sauces (also known by their Italian name *zabaglione*) are another form of emulsion sauce, and are made with egg yolks, wine and sugar.

VARIATIONS OF HOLLANDAISE SAUCE

Béarnaise: This is essentially a hollandaise sauce with 30 ml chopped tarragon added to the reduction. Replace the white wine vinegar with the same amount of tarragon vinegar. Add another 15 ml of chopped fresh tarragon just before serving. Serve with grilled meat.

Horseradish Béarnaise: Add 30 ml creamed horseradish to the finished Béarnaise sauce. Serve with grilled steak or grilled salmon.

Variations of Hollandaise Sauce continue on page 50

BASIC RECIPE 21

Hollandaise Sauce

Makes 300–350 ml

100 ml	white wine vinegar
200 ml	white wine
6	white peppercorns, crushed
1	sprig fresh thyme
2	shallots, finely chopped
3	free-range egg yolks
225 ml	Clarified Butter (*Basic Recipe 10, page 39*), warmed
	salt
	freshly ground pepper
	juice of ½ lemon

Place the white wine vinegar, white wine, crushed peppercorns, thyme and chopped shallots into a heavy-based saucepan over medium heat and reduce by half.

Remove from the heat and pass the liquid through a fine sieve into a clean stainless steel bowl. Allow to cool.

When cold, add the egg yolks. Place the bowl over a pot of simmering water and whisk vigorously to a sabayon until the eggs have doubled in volume and become creamy. Take care that the eggs don't become too hot or they will scramble.

Remove the eggs from the heat and whisk in the clarified butter in a slow, steady stream until it is fully incorporated and the sauce has thickened. Season to taste with salt, freshly ground pepper and lemon juice.

Pass the sauce through a fine sieve into a clean bowl. Cover the bowl with clingfilm. Keep the hollandaise sauce in a warm place until ready to use as the butter will solidify if the sauce becomes cold. If too hot, the butter will separate from the eggs.

Paloise: Make the basic hollandaise, adding some mint stalks to the reduction. Add 30 ml chopped fresh mint just before serving. Serve with lamb.

Choron: Make the basic hollandaise and add 30 ml tomato ketchup to the finished sauce. Serve with grilled steak, lamb, chicken or grilled white fish.

Mousseline Hollandaise: Make the basic hollandaise. Fold in 75 ml lightly whipped cream just before serving. Serve with asparagus or poached fish.

Truffle Hollandaise: Add 20 ml truffle juice to the egg yolks before making the sabayon as on page 49. Once the hollandaise has been passed, add 15 g chopped truffle just before serving.

COMMON PROBLEMS WHEN MAKING EMULSION SAUCES

- The temperature at which the sauce was made was too high, causing the sauce to split.
- The ingredients were not at the correct temperature, causing the sauce to split.
- The fat component of the sauce was added too quickly, causing the sauce to split.
- There was too much fat in the sauce and not enough liquid, causing the sauce to split.

Beurre Blanc and Variations

Hot butter sauces, such as beurre blanc, are traditionally made with a reduction of wine or vinegar with shallots and herbs, and then thickened with butter.

Cold butter sauces are known as compound butters and can be sweet or savoury. These butters are not emulsified, but simply mixed and flavoured with various ingredients from cinnamon to foie gras. They are served cold, placed onto hot food to melt into an instant sauce.

Diced, chilled butter or compound butters are whisked into liquid to thicken. The liquid is reduced to eliminate water and to concentrate flavour and then the butter is whisked into it over a low heat until fully incorporated. Butter sauces must be used immediately as they will split if reheated. If the sauce gets too cold, the butter will solidify.

A classic beurre blanc is made without the addition of cream. However, if you want to hold it for a length of time, a little cream may be added to the reduction to help stabilise the sauce, but it will dilute its buttery flavour slightly. Use a good-quality unsalted butter when adding to sauces and for making clarified and compound butters.

BASIC RECIPE 22

Beurre Blanc

Makes 450 ml

100 ml	**white wine**
50 ml	**white wine vinegar**
1	**large shallot, peeled and sliced**
1	**sprig fresh thyme**
½	**dried bay leaf**

Place the white wine, vinegar, shallot, thyme, bay leaf and crushed peppercorns in a heavy-based saucepan over medium heat and reduce by three-quarters.

Add the cream and bring to the boil, allowing the cream to reduce by half.

6	white peppercorns, crushed
50 ml	fresh cream
225 g	unsalted butter, chilled and diced
	salt
	freshly ground pepper
	lemon juice

Reduce the heat and whisk in the butter, piece-by-piece, until it is fully incorporated into the cream.

Remove from the heat and season to taste with salt, freshly ground pepper and a squeeze of fresh lemon.

Pass the beurre blanc through a fine chinois and keep it warm. Do not re-boil as the sauce will separate. If the sauce gets too cold, the butter will solidify.

VARIATIONS OF BEURRE BLANC

Nantais Beurre Blanc: The beurre blanc recipe is made with equal amounts of vinegar and wine in the reduction to give the sauce a more acidic flavour. This sauce is most commonly served with fish.

Red Wine Beurre Blanc: Replace the white wine with red wine and the white wine vinegar with red wine vinegar and proceed as for the basic beurre blanc. It can be served with either fish or meat. This sauce is perfect served with grilled meats with the addition of a spoonful of reduced veal stock.

Tapenade Beurre Blanc: Whisk 100–120 g tapenade into the beurre blanc to taste. The sauce will take on a charcoal colour. Check the seasoning and adjust if necessary with salt, freshly ground white pepper and a squeeze of lemon. Pass the sauce through a fine chinois and keep warm. Do not re-boil the tapenade beurre blanc as the sauce will separate. If the sauce gets too cold, the butter will solidify.

Herb Beurre Blanc: Add 30 ml chopped flat-leaf parsley, chervil, or sliced tarragon or chives to the finished beurre blanc just before serving (to prevent the herbs from discolouring).

Saffron Beurre Blanc: Add a pinch of saffron threads or powder to the basic beurre blanc reduction before adding the cream. Finish the beurre blanc with a squeeze of fresh lemon and orange juice.

Pesto Beurre Blanc: Add pesto to taste to the finished beurre blanc so that the sauce takes on a deep green colour. Serve with either fish or grilled lamb.

Ginger and Lemon Beurre Blanc: Add 5 ml freshly grated ginger and 2.5 ml finely chopped lemon grass to the reduction before adding the cream. Proceed with the basic recipe and add fresh lemon juice and pickled ginger juice to taste before passing the sauce through a fine chinois. Serve with shellfish or chicken.

COMMON PROBLEMS WHEN MAKING BEURRE BLANC

- The butter was added too quickly, causing the sauce to split.
- The butter was too soft and the fats separated in the sauce.
- Too much butter was added and diluted the flavour of the sauce.
- The liquid component of the sauce was reduced too much and there was not enough liquid for the butter to emulsify.
- The sauce is too thin because the reduction was not reduced enough or not enough butter was added to thicken the sauce.
- The cream used in the sauce was too old and separated when heated.
- Too much acidity in the sauce, such as lemon juice, results in overpowering the intended flavour of the sauce.
- The sauce was made at too high a temperature, causing the butter to separate.
- The sauce went cold and the butter solidified, splitting when reheated.

Picture on next page

VILUX
WINE VINEGAR

Compound Butters and Variations

Flavourings such as herbs, lemon, foie gras and truffle are added to softened butter, which is then rolled tightly in greaseproof paper and frozen. They make an instant sauce when sliced and served with a piece of grilled fish or meat, or they can be whisked into a liquid to thicken and add flavour.

When making compound butters, ensure that the butter is at room temperature. Chop all the flavouring ingredients finely before adding. Once the butter has been mixed, allow it to stand at room temperature for 1 hour before rolling and freezing to allow the flavour to permeate the butter. Compound butters will keep for 3 months in the freezer. Use a good-quality unsalted butter.

BASIC RECIPE 23

Café de Paris Butter

Makes 1.25 kg

3 g	dried marjoram (approx. 2.5 ml)
3 g	dried thyme (approx. 2.5 ml)
2 g	dried oregano (approx. 2.5 ml)
50 g	brown onion, chopped finely
50 g	shallot, chopped finely
10 g	garlic, chopped finely
25 g	Maldon sea salt
75 ml	white wine
10 ml	cognac
1 kg	unsalted butter
3	free-range eggs
10 g	ground white pepper
10 ml	fresh lemon juice
10 ml	Worcestershire sauce
15 ml	sambal oelek
5 ml	pesto
50 g	curly-leaf parsley, chopped

In a heavy-based saucepan, mix together the dried herbs, onions, shallot, garlic, salt, white wine and cognac. Bring to the boil, reduce the heat to a simmer and cook for 10 minutes. Remove from the heat and allow to go cold.

Beat the butter with an electric mixer until light and airy.

Beat the eggs, pepper, lemon juice, Worcestershire sauce, sambal oelek and pesto together. Add the cold reduction and chopped parsley and mix through. Ladle the herb mixture into the butter and continue to beat until it is fully incorporated.

Lay a sheet of greaseproof paper on a work surface and spoon the butter down the centre of the paper. Fold the paper over and roll the butter into a long cylinder shape. Roll the butter in a sheet of aluminium foil and roll up tightly. Place the butter in the freezer and slice as needed.

Foie Gras Butter

Makes approximately 200 g

100 g	unsalted butter
100 g	cooked foie gras
15 ml	brandy
	Maldon sea salt
	freshly ground pepper

Bring the butter and foie gras to room temperature and pass them through a drum sieve. Mix together until smooth and the foie gras is evenly distributed through the butter. Stir in the brandy and season to taste with salt and freshly ground pepper.

Roquefort Butter

Makes approximately 250 g

50 g	crumbled Roquefort
200 g	softened, unsalted butter
	freshly ground white pepper

Add the Roquefort to the butter and season with freshly ground white pepper.

Garlic and Herb Butter

Makes approximately 375 g

250 g	unsalted butter at room temperature
12	cloves garlic, roasted and puréed
50 g	flat-leaf parsley, chopped
45 ml	sliced garlic chives
	Maldon sea salt
	freshly ground white pepper
	fresh lemon juice

Place the butter in a mixing bowl and beat until light and fluffy.

Place the garlic and herbs into a blender with 15 ml of the softened butter and blend until the chlorophyll is released from the herbs and the butter is a deep green colour.

Add the puréed herbs to the butter in the mixing bowl and mix until the herbs are evenly distributed. Season to taste with salt, freshly ground white pepper and lemon juice.

Cep Butter

Makes approximately 250 g

10 g	dried cep mushrooms
150 ml	warm water
50 ml	Madeira wine
200 g	softened, unsalted butter
30 ml	finely chopped flat-leaf parsley
	salt
	freshly ground white pepper

Soak the mushrooms in the warm water and Madeira wine for 1 hour.

Place in a saucepan over low heat and cook for 10 minutes. Remove the mushrooms and allow to cool.

Return the liquid to the heat and gently reduce to a syrup. Chop the cep mushrooms finely and mix through the butter until evenly distributed. Pass the reduced liquid through a fine chinois and add to the butter.

Add the parsley and season to taste with salt and freshly ground white pepper.

Smoked Paprika Butter

Makes approximately 200 g

	smoked paprika
	lemon juice
200 g	softened, unsalted butter

Add smoked paprika to taste and a squeeze of fresh lemon juice to the butter.

Wholegrain Mustard Butter

Makes approximately 215 g

	wholegrain mustard
200 g	**softened, unsalted butter**
30 ml	**finely chopped tarragon**
	lemon juice
	salt
	freshly ground pepper

Add wholegrain mustard to taste to the butter. Add the tarragon and a squeeze of fresh lemon juice. Season to taste with salt and freshly ground pepper.

Herb Butter

Makes approximately 150 g

125 g	**unsalted butter, diced**
6	**cloves Garlic Confit, puréed and passed through a fine sieve (*page 188*)**
45 ml	**finely chopped flat-leaf parsley**
30 ml	**finely sliced chives**
15 ml	**finely chopped tarragon**
	salt
	freshly ground pepper
	fresh lemon juice

Allow the butter to soften at room temperature. Place the garlic and herbs into a food processor and blend. Add the butter gradually until it has all been added and the herbs and garlic are fully incorporated. Remove the butter and season to taste with salt, freshly ground pepper and a squeeze of fresh lemon.

Deep-Fried Herb Butter

Makes 8 pieces

150 g	**Herb Butter (see recipe above)**
	egg wash of 1 egg and 10 ml milk
50 g	**fresh breadcrumbs**
	vegetable oil for deep-frying
	salt
	freshly ground pepper

Allow the herb butter to soften at room temperature. Using two warm teaspoons, make quenelles of the butter and place them on a clingfilm-lined tray. Place the tray in the freezer until the quenelles of butter are frozen.

To prepare the quenelles for frying, place into the egg wash, drain and dip into the breadcrumbs. Repeat the process so that the butter is double-crumbed. Heat the oil to 180 °C and deep-fry the butter until the quenelles are golden. Remove the deep-fried herb butter from the oil and drain. Lightly season with salt and freshly ground pepper.

OILS, VINAIGRETTES AND DRESSINGS

Vinaigrettes and Dressings

Vinaigrette is a simple mixture of two or three parts oil mixed with one part vinegar and/or lemon juice, and seasoned with salt, spices and herbs. It can vary from sweet or tangy to more herbed or spicy; it can be creamy or oily.

Vinaigrettes are customarily used as salad dressings, but these simple sauces also add great flavour to vegetables, meat, game, poultry, fish and shellfish and can be used as both a marinade and dressing for dishes such as escabèche and ceviche.

All vinaigrettes begin with the same ingredients: good-quality vinegar and oil. However, they can be easily changed with different vinegars, oils, spices, herbs, flavourings and seasoning, depending on the desired taste and purpose of the sauce. The different ingredients and spices that can be added will influence the flavour it imparts to food. You can use vinegars such as sherry, balsamic, white wine, red wine, champagne, cider and verjuice – to name just a few. Other ingredients such as parsley, garlic, shallot, mustard, citrus, coriander seeds and saffron will give you a vast range of flavours and combinations. For example, you could use extra virgin olive oil, lemon juice and seasoning to make light vinaigrette, or rice wine vinegar, sesame oil, ginger and lime for a more complex Asian vinaigrette. The combination of flavours is endless.

Dressings with acidic ingredients should not be kept in containers with metal lids but rather transferred to glass containers with airtight lids.

Oils

Olive oil is an essential ingredient in any kitchen, but when it comes to making dressings and vinaigrettes there are plenty of other fruit and nut oils that can be used. Most oils will keep for months once opened if they are kept in a cool, dark place.

Unlike many wines, oils do not benefit from ageing, so it is best to buy in small quantities. Once a bottle has been opened it should be used within a month or two. Heat and light both affect the quality of oil so buy oil either in a dark bottle, tins or ceramic containers. Once opened it can be refrigerated to prevent it from oxidising and brought back to room temperature before using. Like all other fats, olive oil will deteriorate during the frying process, especially at high temperature. Use a less expensive and less fruity olive oil for cooking.

When selecting an olive oil to use for dressings and vinaigrettes, choose one that has been produced from a single estate. These are the best oils produced from olives grown on a single estate, usually picked by hand, pressed and bottled on site.

Hazelnut oil is fragrant and full-flavoured, with a slightly sweet, roasted taste. Walnut oil is produced from different varieties of walnuts with high oil content. Once harvested, the walnuts are stored for 2–3 months to allow their milky juices to transform into clear oil before being pressed. Not normally served on their own, these oils are used as a flavouring in dressings, sauces and pastries. Use the best quality oils you can find. The oil should be bought in small quantities and refrigerated once opened as they have a short shelf life.

Truffle-infused oils should be carefully chosen as some are chemically enhanced and should be avoided. Look for truffle oil that has slivers of truffle infusing in it and use in moderation as they are very strong and intense in flavour and can overpower a dish.

Peanut oil is very pale in colour, with a light consistency and an exceptionally high smoking point, making it an excellent choice for all types of frying. Chinese peanut oils are best, as they have a distinctive peanut taste. It is a great all-purpose oil.

There are two varieties of sesame oil: a light, mild one that is cold pressed from white sesame seeds, and a darker and stronger flavoured one extracted from roasted sesame seeds. Sesame oil has a very distinctive, nutty flavour and is mainly used in Asian cooking, not only to cook with but also for flavouring. Sesame oil is often blended with more neutral oils, such as peanut or grape seed oils, to dilute the strong flavour.

Safflower oil is a light oil made from safflowers – a relative of the sunflower – and is a healthy oil with almost no flavour. It is good for sautéing or pan-frying.

Vinegars

The word 'vinegar' is a combination of the French words *vin* and *aigre* and literally means 'sour wine'. Vinegar is a solution of acetic acid created through fermentation and can be made from most foodstuffs that contain natural sugars. Naturally occurring yeasts convert the sugars into alcohol, then bacteria transforms the alcohol into vinegar. Though all vinegars share the common flavour of acetic acid, each retains the distinctive flavour of the alcohol mixture from which it was started, and some, such as sherry and balsamic, develop flavour and colour from being fermented or aged in barrels.

Wine vinegar is fermented from grape wine and has a sweet, fruity flavour. Generic wine vinegars are either white or red, and speciality wine vinegars might specify a particular grape or wine, such as chardonnay, cabernet sauvignon or sherry.

Champagne vinegar is classically made in the Champagne region of France. It is usually the lightest of the vinegars.

Sherry vinegar is wine vinegar made from the famous fortified wine of southern Spain. Like sherry itself, sherry vinegar is aged using the solera system (where younger vinegars are mingled with older vinegars in a pyramid of oak barrels). Sherry vinegar has a caramel and almond-like quality similar to that of sherry. It is a great vinegar to deglaze a pan for a quick sauce for sautéed chicken, veal or pork.

Balsamic vinegar has been produced in Modena in the Bologna region of Italy for centuries. Any vinegar originating from this area is sold under a label of authenticity that makes it superior to the cheaper factory-produced balsamic that often has the addition of caramel to enhance the colour and taste. Balsamic vinegar is produced by boiling the must of late-harvested, white Trebbiano grapes, until it is reduced by half. These grapes have a high sugar content. The boiled must is then transferred to, and aged in, wooden casks. The temperature of the different seasons plays an important role in the process; during the hot summer months the heat causes the balsamic to evaporate and concentrate, and in the colder months it rests and matures. As the vinegar ages it is siphoned from barrel to barrel of decreasing size. The different woods used in these barrels – oak, chestnut, cherry, ash and mulberry – each impart distinctive flavours to the vinegar. The ageing process can take up to 10 years and as long as 50 years. As the vinegar ages it becomes richer, sweeter, syrupy and more expensive. It can be used in both sweet and savoury dishes and the older vinegars should be used very sparingly. The sweetness from balsamic vinegar makes it ideal to use with bitter salad leaves such as radicchio and chicory, or with fresh fruits such as strawberries and figs.

Vinegars are extremely stable and can be kept indefinitely. Store vinegar in a glass or ceramic container, and seal it with plastic or cork. Never store vinegar in metal, which will corrode.

BASIC RECIPE 24

À la Grecque Vinaigrette

Makes 500 ml

100 ml	Champagne vinegar
250 ml	water or Chicken Stock (*Basic Recipe 1, page 12*)
150 ml	extra virgin olive oil
	juice of 1 lemon
1	dried bay leaf
	pinch saffron threads
1	sprig fresh rosemary
1	sprig fresh thyme
4	cloves garlic, crushed
20	white peppercorns
20	coriander seeds
	pinch Maldon sea salt

Combine all the ingredients in a heavy-based saucepan and simmer over a low heat for 20 minutes.

Remove from the heat and allow to cool. Remove the rosemary, thyme, bay leaf and garlic and discard.

Store in a parfait jar and refrigerate until ready to use.

Variations of À la Grecque

Lemon à la Grecque

Makes 200 ml

10	lemons
200 ml	À la Grecque Vinaigrette (*Basic Recipe 25, see above*)

Wash the lemons under cold running water. Remove the peel using a swivel peeler to obtain wide strips of peel. Using a sharp, thin-bladed knife remove all the pith from the peel. Trim the sides of the peel and cut them into 5 mm dice.

Place the diced lemon peel in a heavy-based saucepan and add the À la Grecque Vinaigrette. Place over a very low heat and cook until the lemon peel softens, about 1 hour. Remove from the heat and allow to cool, leaving the lemon in the vinaigrette. Store in a parfait jar and refrigerate until ready to use.

Alternatively, the lemons can be sliced into thin rounds with the skin on and cooked in the same manner.

Mushroom à la Grecque

Serves 4

200 ml	**À la Grecque Vinaigrette (*Basic Recipe 24, page 61*)**
25 ml	**olive oil**
150 g	**button mushrooms**
50 g	**oyster mushrooms**
50 g	**shimiji mushrooms**
	salt
	freshly ground pepper
15 ml	**sliced chives**
15 ml	**chopped tarragon**
15 ml	**chopped flat-leaf parsley**

Warm the À la Grecque Vinaigrette in a heavy-based saucepan over a low heat.

In a separate heavy-based pan, heat the olive oil and sauté all the mushrooms until golden brown. Drain the mushrooms, transfer to a bowl and pour over the warm À la Grecque Vinaigrette. Season to taste with salt and freshly ground pepper.

Store in a parfait jar and refrigerate until ready to use.

Add the herbs just before serving to avoid the vinegar from discolouring them.

In addition to the varieties listed, any type of mushroom can be used, such as cep, morel or trompette.

Vegetable à la Grecque

Serves 4

Use a selection of fresh, seasonal vegetables. The Vegetable à la Grecque can be served either warm or at room temperature, as an entrée or as a garnish to grilled or poached fish.

200 ml	**À la Grecque Vinaigrette (*Basic Recipe 24, page 61*)**
25 ml	**olive oil**
	selection of mixed mushrooms
1	**small fennel bulb, thinly sliced**
8	**baby potatoes, boiled, peeled and halved**
1	**red pepper, blanched and peeled (*Basic Technique 15, page 180*)**
1	**yellow pepper, blanched and peeled (*Basic Technique 15, page 180*)**
2	**vine-ripened tomatoes, blanched, peeled, quartered and seeded)**
4	**spears asparagus, peeled and blanched (*Basic Technique 17, page 184*)**
50 g	**fresh peas, blanched and refreshed**
	salt
	freshly ground pepper
15 ml	**sliced chives**
15 ml	**chopped tarragon**
15 ml	**chopped flat-leaf parsley**

Warm the à la Grecque vinaigrette in a heavy-based saucepan over low heat.

In a separate heavy-based pan, heat the olive oil and sauté the mushrooms until golden brown. Drain the mushrooms, transfer to a bowl, add the remaining vegetables and pour over the warm à la Grecque vinaigrette. Season to taste with salt and freshly ground pepper.

Store in a parfait jar and refrigerate until ready to use.

Add the herbs just before serving to avoid the vinegar from discolouring them.

In addition to the varieties listed, any type of vegetable can be used, such as artichokes, courgettes, baby carrots or snow peas.

BASIC RECIPE 25

Mayonnaise

Makes 500 ml

The eggs in mayonnaise hold the oil in suspension, while vinegar and lemon add acidity and flavour. A well-prepared base sauce opens up many possibilities for a selection of variations. Do not use olive oil to make mayonnaise as its flavour is too strong and overpowering.

When mayonnaise separates, it is due to one of the following: the oil was added too quickly to the egg; the oil was too cold; or the quantity of oil was too great for the amount of egg used. Bring all ingredients to room temperature before making mayonnaise. If the sauce does split, place a fresh egg yolk with a spoonful of mustard in a bowl and beat together, then slowly whisk in the curdled sauce, adding a little at a time. If the mayonnaise becomes too thick, add a little warm water to thin it out.

2	free-range egg yolks
15 ml	Dijon mustard
30 ml	white wine vinegar
	dash Worcestershire sauce
500 ml	peanut oil
	salt
	freshly ground pepper
1	lemon

Place the egg yolks, mustard, vinegar and Worcestershire sauce in a bowl and whisk until pale and doubled in volume.

Add the oil in a slow, steady stream so that the egg yolk absorbs the oil. Continue to whisk until all the oil has been incorporated. Season to taste with salt, freshly ground pepper and a squeeze of lemon juice.

If the mayonnaise is too thick, thin it out with a dash of warm water. Cover with clingfilm and refrigerate until ready to use.

Variations of Mayonnaise

Sauce Tartare

Makes 300 ml

250 ml	Mayonnaise (*Basic Recipe 25, see above*)
30 g	capers, rinsed and finely chopped
30 g	gherkins, finely chopped
15 ml	chopped herbs, equal quantities of parsley, chive, tarragon and chervil
	salt
	freshly ground pepper
1	lemon

Place the mayonnaise in a bowl. Fold in the capers, gherkins and chopped herbs. Season to taste with salt, freshly ground pepper and a squeeze of fresh lemon juice. Refrigerate until ready to use.

LEA

Sauce Rémoulade

Makes 300 ml

300 ml	Mayonnaise (*Basic Recipe 25, page 64*)
5 ml	chopped tinned anchovy fillet
30 ml	chopped French tarragon

Place the mayonnaise in a bowl. Fold in the chopped anchovy and tarragon.

Aïoli

Makes 250 ml

250 ml	Mayonnaise (*Basic Recipe 25, page 64*)
8	cloves slow-roasted garlic, puréed and passed through a fine sieve (*page 188*)
	salt
	freshly ground pepper

Place the mayonnaise in a bowl. Fold in the garlic purée to taste. Adjust the seasoning if necessary.

Cocktail Sauce or Marie Rose Sauce

Makes 300 ml

250 ml	Mayonnaise (*Basic Recipe 25, page 64*)
40–50 ml	tomato ketchup (enough to turn the sauce light orange in colour)
	orange juice
	dash brandy
	pinch paprika
	salt
	freshly ground pepper

Place the mayonnaise in a bowl. Whisk in the tomato ketchup until evenly incorporated. Season to taste with a squeeze of fresh orange juice, brandy, paprika, salt and freshly ground pepper.

Sauce Rouille

Makes 250 ml

250 ml	Mayonnaise (*Basic Recipe 25, page 64*)
5 ml	tomato paste
	pinch saffron threads
1	red chilli, seeded and finely chopped
	pinch cayenne pepper

Place the mayonnaise in a bowl. Whisk in the tomato paste, saffron and red chilli. The sauce should have a rusty colour. Season to taste with cayenne pepper.

Thousand Island Sauce

Makes 350 ml

250 ml	Mayonnaise (*Basic Recipe 25, page 64*)
40–50 ml	tomato ketchup (enough to turn the sauce light orange in colour)
1	shallot, finely chopped
25 g	diced red pepper
25 g	diced green pepper
	orange juice
	dash brandy
	pinch paprika
	salt
	freshly ground pepper

Place the mayonnaise in a bowl. Whisk in the tomato ketchup until evenly incorporated. Fold in the shallot and peppers. Season to taste with a squeeze of fresh orange juice, brandy, paprika, salt and freshly ground pepper.

Avocado Sauce

Makes 300 ml

250 ml	Mayonnaise (*Basic Recipe 25, page 64*)
1	avocado
	lemon juice
	pinch cayenne pepper
	salt
	freshly ground pepper

Place the mayonnaise in a bowl. Blend the avocado in a food processor with a squeeze of fresh lemon juice. Fold the avocado through the mayonnaise and season to taste with cayenne pepper, salt, freshly ground pepper and a squeeze of fresh lemon juice.

BASIC RECIPE 26

Basil Oil

Makes 400 ml

150 g	fresh basil leaves
350 ml	extra virgin olive oil
2	cloves garlic, peeled and finely chopped
	salt
	freshly ground pepper
	lemon juice

Blanch the basil leaves in boiling water for 15 seconds and refresh in iced water. Drain the basil and dry on a clean tea towel to absorb any excess water.

Pour 50 ml olive oil into a blender and, with the motor running, add the garlic. Blend to a purée.

Feed the basil into the blender. Pour in the remaining oil and continue to blend until smooth. Season to taste with salt, freshly ground pepper and a squeeze of fresh lemon juice.

Pour the basil purée into a sieve lined with a double layer of muslin cloth set over a bowl to collect the oil. When the oil has drained, discard the pulp.

Store the basil oil in a sealed bottle and refrigerate until ready to use.

BASIC RECIPE 27

Lemon Oil

Makes 1 litre

20	lemons
5 ml	salt
15 ml	sugar
500 ml	grape seed oil
500 ml	extra virgin olive oil

Wash the lemons and remove the zest over a large bowl to catch all the spray released from the peel.

Dissolve the salt and sugar in the juice of 2 of the lemons in a heavy-based saucepan. Add the oils and lemon zest. Place over a very low heat and gently warm the oil.

Remove from the heat and allow the lemon zest to infuse the oil for 24 hours.

Pass it through a sieve lined with a double layer of muslin cloth. Discard the zest.

Store the lemon oil in a sealed bottle and refrigerate until ready to use.

BASIC RECIPE 28

Crustacean Oil

Makes 750 ml

700 g	prawn or lobster shells and heads, crushed
750 ml	extra virgin olive oil
100 g	tomato paste
2	cloves garlic
2	star anise
2	red chillies, split and seeded
12	white peppercorns, crushed
12	coriander seeds, crushed
2	sprigs fresh thyme
2	sprigs fresh tarragon
2	dried bay leaves
	pinch Maldon sea salt
	freshly ground pepper

Preheat the oven to 130 °C.

Clean and chop the shells into small pieces.

Heat 50 ml extra virgin olive oil in a roasting tray and add the shells. Transfer to the oven and roast for 1–1½ hours, stirring frequently until the shells become dry, brittle and deeply coloured.

Stir the tomato paste into the shells so that they are evenly coated. Return to the oven and continue to roast for a further 15 minutes, stirring from time to time.

Remove from the oven and add the garlic, star anise, chillies, peppercorns, coriander seeds, herbs and a pinch of Maldon sea salt and freshly ground pepper. Mix through the roasted shells.

Spoon the mix into a sterilised Kilner jar and pour the remaining extra virgin olive oil over the shells, filling the jar right to the top.

Place the jar in a large saucepan and surround it with a tea towel to prevent it from knocking the sides. Pour in enough water to come three-quarters of the way up the side of the jar. Bring the water to the boil, reduce the heat to a simmer and cook for 45 minutes.

Carefully remove the jar from the water and allow it to cool before placing it in the fridge. The longer it is stored in the fridge, the more intense both the flavour and colour of the oil will become.

When ready to use, pass the oil through a sieve lined with a double layer of muslin cloth and adjust the seasoning if necessary.

Picture on page 70

BASIC RECIPE 29

Parmesan Oil

Makes 250 ml

Save Parmesan rinds to make this simple infused oil. Use it as a simple sauce to dress pasta or freshly cooked vegetables such as peas or cauliflower, or pour it over roasted potatoes. It is important that the Parmesan rinds are covered with oil because they will go mouldy if exposed to air. When not using, keep the oil refrigerated to extend its shelf life.

50 g	Parmesan rinds
3	cloves garlic, peeled and crushed
4	sprigs fresh thyme
4	white peppercorns, crushed
250 ml	extra virgin olive oil

Place the Parmesan rinds into a glass jar. Add the garlic, thyme and crushed peppercorns. Cover with the olive oil and allow to infuse for 48 hours before using. The Parmesan oil may be topped up with oil a second time.

BASIC RECIPE 30

Tomato Oil

Makes 600 ml

300 ml	extra virgin olive oil
2	cloves garlic, peeled and finely chopped
½	small onion, finely chopped
2	shallots, finely chopped
1	stick celery, finely chopped
½	bulb fennel, finely chopped
1	small leek, white part only, finely chopped
½	red chilli, seeded and finely chopped
40 ml	tomato paste
2	sprigs fresh thyme
½	dried bay leaf
1	sprig fresh rosemary
4	white peppercorns, crushed
6	coriander seeds, crushed
300 ml	grape seed oil
1	small bunch fresh basil, picked and roughly chopped
	salt
	freshly ground pepper

Heat 50 ml extra virgin olive oil in a heavy-based pan over medium heat, and add the garlic and chopped vegetables. Sweat for 5 minutes without colour until tender.

Add the tomato paste, thyme, bay leaf, rosemary, peppercorns and coriander seeds and continue to cook for a further 5 minutes. Stir to prevent the tomato paste from sticking. Add the remaining olive oil and the grape seed oil and continue to cook over very low heat for 1 hour.

Remove the oil from the heat, refrigerate and allow to cool before adding the basil. Allow the basil to infuse the oil for 24 hours.

Pass through a sieve lined with a double layer of muslin cloth set over a bowl to collect the oil. When the oil has drained, discard the vegetables. Adjust the seasoning if necessary.

Store the tomato oil in a sealed bottle and refrigerate until ready to use.

home made
CRUSTACEA
OIL
A classic recipe.

Kitchen Craft
home made
CRUSTACEA
OIL
15 FEB '11
A classic recipe Enjoy!

BASIC RECIPE 31

Classic Vinaigrette

Makes 200 ml

Vinaigrette is a simple mixture of two or three parts oil mixed with one part vinegar and/or lemon juice or verjuice, and seasoned with salt, freshly ground pepper, spices and herbs. A vinaigrette recipe is unique to the person who makes it – everyone favours different proportions and additions. Let your palate be your guide. Use any type of vinegar or oil and add optional ingredients such as herbs, citrus juice and spices, from white pepper to saffron or basil to Vietnamese mint.

50 ml Champagne vinegar
150 ml extra virgin olive oil
5 ml Dijon mustard
juice of ½ lemon
salt
freshly ground white pepper

Simply shake everything together in a screw-top jar. Adjust the seasoning if necessary.

VARIATIONS OF SIMPLE VINAIGRETTES

Blackberry vinegar and walnut oil.

Red wine vinegar, extra virgin olive oil, lemon juice, peeled and chopped shallots, crushed garlic, salt and freshly ground pepper.

Champagne vinegar, extra virgin olive oil, lemon juice, runny honey, freshly picked thyme leaves, salt and freshly ground pepper.

Two parts rice wine vinegar, 2 parts sesame oil, 5 parts peanut oil, 1 stick finely chopped lemon grass, 2 cm piece peeled and grated fresh ginger, and fresh lime juice to taste.

BASIC RECIPE 32

Red Wine and Shallot Vinaigrette

Makes 500 ml

This is a very sharp, classical vinaigrette that is served with freshly shucked oysters (*Basic Technique 4, page 100*).

125 g shallots, peeled and finely chopped
150 ml good-quality red wine vinegar
5 ml castor sugar
550 ml red wine
70 ml port
30 ml water
salt
freshly ground pepper

Place the shallots, red wine vinegar and sugar together in a heavy-based saucepan over medium heat. Cook for 3 minutes, then remove from the heat and set aside.

Place the red wine, port and water in a separate heavy-based saucepan over medium heat and reduce by two-thirds. Pour the reduced alcohol over the shallots and season to taste with salt and freshly ground pepper. Refrigerate until ready to serve.

BASIC RECIPE 33

Bois Boudran

Makes 400 ml

This is a strong flavoured vinaigrette that complements grilled or steamed fish, roast chicken or steamed or boiled vegetables such as asparagus, broccoli and artichokes.

75 ml	walnut oil
75 ml	peanut oil
50 ml	cabernet sauvignon vinegar
45 ml	tomato ketchup
5 ml	Worcestershire sauce
	Tabasco sauce
100 g	shallots, chopped
	salt
	freshly ground pepper
100 g	Tomato Concassée (*Basic Technique 13, page 177*)
15 ml	sliced chives
15 ml	sliced tarragon

Whisk together the walnut and peanut oils. Add the cabernet sauvignon vinegar, tomato ketchup, Worcestershire sauce, Tabasco and the shallots. Season to taste with salt and freshly ground pepper.

Just before serving, add the Tomato Concassée and the chopped herbs to prevent them from becoming discoloured.

BASIC RECIPE 34

Roast Tomato Vinaigrette

Makes 550 ml

150 ml	olive oil
½	small onion, peeled and roughly chopped
3	cloves garlic, peeled and thinly sliced
1 kg	overripe vine-ripened tomatoes
3	sprigs fresh thyme
	balsamic vinegar
	salt
	freshly ground pepper
25 g	sun-dried tomatoes
15 ml	tomato paste
250 ml	extra virgin olive oil
	Worcestershire sauce
1	small bunch fresh basil, roughly chopped

Preheat the oven to 180 °C.

Pour the olive oil into a roasting tray and add the onion, garlic, vine-ripened tomatoes and thyme. Drizzle with balsamic vinegar and lightly season with salt and freshly ground pepper. Place in the oven and roast for about 30 minutes, or until the tomato skins begin to blister and burst, releasing their juices.

Stir in the sun-dried tomatoes and tomato paste and continue to cook for a further 10 minutes.

Tip the contents of the roasting tray into a large bowl and whisk in the extra virgin olive oil. Add the Worcestershire sauce and more balsamic vinegar to taste. Add the basil, cover the bowl with clingfilm and allow the flavours to infuse for 1 hour.

Pass the dressing through a fine chinois, pressing down on the tomatoes to extract as much flavour and colour as possible. Adjust the seasoning if necessary. Refrigerate until ready to use.

BASIC RECIPE 35

Rice Wine Vinegar Dressing

Makes 225 ml

110 ml	rice wine vinegar
110 ml	water
65 g	sugar
25 g	fresh ginger root, peeled and sliced
½	red chilli, split
½	clove garlic, peeled and sliced
	salt

Place all the ingredients together in a heavy-based saucepan over low heat and simmer until the sugar has dissolved. Remove from the heat and allow to go cold. Pass the dressing through a fine sieve and discard the ginger, chilli and garlic. Refrigerate until ready to use.

BASIC RECIPE 36

Marinated Olives

Makes 500 g

500 g	kalamata olives
300 ml	extra virgin olive oil
3	cloves garlic, peeled and crushed
2	red chillies, split
5 ml	fennel seeds, lightly roasted
5 ml	coriander seeds, crushed
	zest of 1 orange, cut in strips
1	sprig fresh rosemary
2	sprigs fresh lemon thyme
2	dried bay leaves

Drain the olives, place in a sieve and rinse under cold running water. Dry gently on a clean tea towel.

In a large bowl, mix the remaining ingredients together. Add the olives and stir into the marinade, ensuring the olives are covered in the oil. Store in the fridge, covered tightly. The olives will keep for up to one month.

BASIC RECIPE 37

Tapenade

Makes 150 g

125 g	pitted, ripe black olives
10 g	marinated anchovy fillets
20 g	capers, rinsed
½	clove garlic, crushed
10–15 ml	extra virgin olive oil
	freshly ground pepper
15 ml	chopped flat-leaf parsley

Purée the olives, anchovies, capers and garlic in a food processor to a smooth paste. Add the extra virgin olive oil and blend until incorporated.

Remove the tapenade from the food processor and season with the freshly ground pepper – salt is not needed as the anchovies and capers are salty enough.

Spoon the tapenade into an airtight jar, cover with a thin layer of extra virgin olive oil and refrigerate. Spoon out as required and add freshly chopped parsley to taste just before serving.

SALADS

Lettuce is cultivated in many varieties for its edible leaves, different textures and flavours. When selecting leaves for a salad, pick those that will complement the meal with which they are being served, as different salad leaves have distinct flavours and can be overpowering, such as bitter chicory, curly endive or radicchio or the strong flavour of peppery watercress. Dress salads with an appropriate dressing that isn't overpowered by the salad leaves, just like you would pair a hot sauce with a piece of fish or meat. A delicate truffle or an Asian dressing would be lost with a bitter leaf such as radicchio whereas a Roquefort dressing would complement and stand up to it.

Trim the stems from salad leaves and discard any wilted outer leaves before washing briefly in cold salted water. Drain well and dry on a clean tea towel before dressing to avoid excess water diluting the dressing.

Salad leaves have a waterproof, waxy covering – the cuticle – that makes water roll off them so they don't become sodden. Oil on the other hand is quickly absorbed into the empty spaces in the interior of the leaf, making it wilt and discolour quickly. Oil-based dressings are especially damaging to salad leaves. A salad should be tossed with the chosen dressing just before serving; if done too far in advance, any green leaves will become limp and soggy. There should only be sufficient dressing to lubricate and moisten the ingredients, not enough to leave a pool in the base of the salad bowl. Extra dressing can always be served separately. If you are adding herbs to a salad, rather scatter them over the salad as a garnish to get the full impact of their flavour.

As vegetables are mostly served raw in salads, chop or grate vegetables into small pieces or slice thinly on a mandoline to achieve maximum flavour. Wash and peel all vegetables being used in a salad, except for mushrooms – they just need a wipe with a damp cloth. Salt draws moisture from fresh vegetables. By sprinkling shredded cabbage for coleslaw or cucumber slices with salt before tossing them with a dressing, most of the water in these vegetables can be eliminated so it does not dilute the dressing. Place the vegetables in a colander and lightly salt them. Allow to stand for 10 minutes for the water to be drawn from them. Transfer the vegetables to a clean tea towel and gently pat dry. The salt will have dissolved and drained away with the water.

Balsamic Figs with Prosciutto and Celeriac Rémoulade

Serves 4

Figs are one of the few fruits I would serve with savoury dishes. As the celeriac is served raw, it is important that it is sliced as thinly as possible to enhance the texture of the dish and also to be able to digest it easily.

50 ml	**Sugar Syrup (*Basic Recipe 53, page 229*)**
25 ml	**port**
25 ml	**balsamic vinegar**
½	**stick cinnamon**
2	**star anise**
6	**black figs**
1	**small bulb celeriac**
1	**lemon**
	salt
100 ml	**Mayonnaise (*Basic Recipe 25, page 64*)**
1	**small bunch flat-leaf parsley, finely sliced**
	freshly ground pepper
50 ml	**extra virgin olive oil**
24	**paper-thin slices prosciutto or cured loin of pork**

Put the sugar syrup, port, balsamic vinegar, cinnamon and star anise together in a heavy-based saucepan and bring to the boil. Reduce the heat to a simmer and reduce by a quarter. Remove from the heat and allow to cool.

Prick the figs all over with a fork and place into the syrup to macerate for 6 hours.

Remove the figs from the liquid. Preheat the oven to 200 °C.

Peel and discard the thick outer layer from the celeriac. Slice the celeriac as thinly as possible using an electric slicing machine or a mandoline. Cut the slices into julienne. Place the celeriac into iced water with a squeeze of lemon juice and a pinch of salt to prevent it from becoming discoloured. (The iced water will keep the celeriac crisp as you prepare the rest of the dish.)

Drain the celeriac and dry well in a clean tea towel. Place the celeriac in a bowl and bind it together with the mayonnaise. Add the flat-leaf parsley and mix so that it is evenly distributed through the celeriac. Season to taste with salt and freshly ground pepper and a squeeze of lemon juice.

Using a sharp knife, halve the figs and brush them with a little of the syrup. Place into a roasting pan and roast until the syrup caramelises and the figs begin to soften slightly.

Whisk the olive oil into the remaining port and balsamic syrup to make a vinaigrette. Adjust the seasoning if necessary.

Spread 6 slices of prosciutto onto each of 4 chilled plates. Spoon the celeriac in the centre of the prosciutto and arrange 3 roasted fig halves around the celeriac. Spoon the vinaigrette over and around the figs.

Serve a bowl of rocket leaves dressed in extra virgin olive oil with a little shaved Parmesan cheese in the centre of the table as an accompaniment.

Cucumber, Ginger and Chilli Salad

Serves 6

In Asian cuisine, salads are often served as a cooling complement to something hot. Thai curry is always served with slices of cucumber; Vietnamese food is served with platters of fresh herbs, raw vegetables, cut citrus and lettuce. Yoghurt salads (raita) are served with Indian curries and pickled vegetables are served with Chinese, Japanese and Korean cuisines. This is a simple salad that can be served as an accompaniment to hot and spicy food.

Dressing

110 ml	**rice wine vinegar**
110 ml	**water**
65 g	**sugar**
25 g	**fresh ginger root, peeled and sliced**
½	**red chilli, split**
½	**clove garlic, peeled and sliced**
	salt

Salad

1	**spring onion, thinly sliced**
½	**red chilli, seeded and thinly sliced**
½	**red onion, peeled and thinly sliced**
2	**slices pickled ginger, thinly sliced**
1	**cucumber**

Place the rice wine vinegar, water, sugar, ginger, chilli, garlic and a pinch of salt together in a heavy-based saucepan over low heat and simmer until the sugar has dissolved. Remove from the heat and allow to go cold.

Place the sliced spring onion, chilli, red onion and pickled ginger together in a bowl and gently mix together. Pass the dressing through a fine sieve over the mixture and discard the ginger, chilli and garlic.

Top and tail the cucumber and cut it in half crossways. Slice the cucumber thinly lengthways with a sharp knife or preferably on a mandoline, discarding the first slice of thick cucumber skin. Add the cucumber to the salad and adjust the seasoning with a pinch of salt if necessary. Refrigerate the salad until ready to serve.

Roast Bone Marrow with Parsley and Shallot Salad

Serves 4

The marrow bone comes from a calf's leg. Ask your butcher to keep some for you. You will need teaspoons to scrape out the marrow and a supply of freshly toasted sourdough bread. With the addition of thinly sliced raw fennel and chopped fronds of fennel, you have a fresh, crisp salad to serve with plain grilled or roasted fish.

12	**7–8 cm pieces marrow bone**
1	**large bunch flat-leaf parsley, picked from its stems**
3	**shallots, peeled and thinly sliced**
25 g	**capers**
30 ml	**extra virgin olive oil**
	juice of 1 lemon
	sea salt
	freshly ground pepper

Preheat the oven to 180 °C.

Wrap the ends of the marrow bones in aluminium foil to prevent any seepage. Put the marrow bones in a roasting tray or ovenproof frying pan and roast for 15–20 minutes, depending on the thickness of the bones. The marrow should loosen from the sides of the bones but not melt away.

Finely slice the parsley and place in a bowl. Add the shallots and capers and mix together. Add the olive oil and lemon juice to taste. Season with salt and freshly ground pepper.

Place the marrow bones on a warmed plate and serve the salad in a bowl with a plate of warm toast.

To eat, scrape the marrow from the bone and spread over a warm piece of toast. Top with a spoonful of parsley salad and a sprinkling of sea salt.

Picture on next page

Smoked Salmon and Crab Sushi Salad

Serves 4

Sushi salad

180 g	**Japanese short grain rice, rinsed**
225 ml	**water**
125 g	**freshly picked white crab meat (*Basic Technique 3, page 98*)**
100 g	**mixed salad leaves, such as pea shoots, mizuna and baby coriander**
2	**red radishes, thinly sliced**
15 ml	**finely sliced pickled ginger**
10 g	**nori seaweed, finely sliced**
200 g	**finely sliced smoked salmon**
15 ml	**flying fish roe**

Sushi vinegar

50 ml	**rice wine vinegar**
7.5 ml	**salt**
4 ml	**mirin**
35 g	**castor sugar**

Chilli dressing

10 ml	**peeled and grated ginger**
5 ml	**finely chopped garlic**
2	**red chillies, seeded and chopped**
22.5 ml	**light sesame oil**
30 ml	**peanut oil**
	juice of 1 lime
22.5 ml	**soy sauce**
5 ml	**sugar**
10 ml	**hot chilli powder**

First make the dressing. Place all of the dressing ingredients in a bowl and whisk together. Refrigerate until ready to use.

Make the sushi vinegar (this can be made in advance and will keep refrigerated for up to a month). In a heavy-based, non-reactive saucepan, gently heat 35 ml of the vinegar with the salt, mirin and sugar until the sugar has dissolved – do not allow the liquid to boil. Remove from the heat and allow to cool completely. When cold, add the remaining vinegar. Set aside until ready to use.

Wash the rice in a large bowl of cold water, rubbing it and rinsing it frequently with fresh water until all the excess starch is gone and the water is clear. Soak the rice in fresh cold water for 30 minutes, and then drain.

Place the rice and the 225 ml of water in a heavy-based saucepan. Bring to the boil over high heat for 1 minute, then reduce the heat to low and continue to cook for a further 5 minutes. Remove the saucepan from the heat and allow to stand for 15 minutes before draining off any excess water.

Transfer the rice to a wide, shallow container and spread out thinly with a wooden spoon. Sprinkle half of the sushi vinegar over the rice and, working quickly in a slicing motion, cut through the rice from the bottom of the tub so that it gets turned over and evenly blends in the vinegar. Take care not to squash the grains of rice or to over-stir them as this will make it become too sticky. Cover the rice with a clean, damp cloth and use while at room temperature within 1 hour. Do not use it if it becomes too cold or too hard.

In a bowl mix the crab meat with the salad leaves, radishes, ginger and seaweed. Add the sushi rice and gently mix through the salad.

Place a lightly oiled ring mould, 7.5 cm in diameter, in the centre of a chilled bowl plate. Line the inner edges with a strip of smoked salmon. Fill the centre with the sushi salad, taking it to the top of the smoked salmon. Carefully remove the ring mould. Top each salad with a little of the fish roe and drizzle the dressing around the smoked salmon.

Salad of Beetroot with Goat's Cheese and Herbs

Serves 4

The photograph shows the exact same ingredients but they are just plated differently. Intricate plating does nothing to improve the flavour but can be detrimental to the final dish. Rather focus on flavour and correct cooking technique than fussy presentation.

8	**medium beetroot**
3 L	**water**
200 ml	**verjuice**
100 ml	**chardonnay vinegar**
	pinch saffron threads
80 g	**sugar**
5 ml	**salt**
	freshly ground pepper
200 g	**soft goat's cheese**
30 ml	**crème fraîche**
15 ml	**Shallot Confit (*page 193*)**
15 ml	**chopped mixed herbs, such as flat-leaf parsley, chervil, tarragon and chives**
	baby beetroot leaves and sorrel leaves to garnish
15 ml	**extra virgin olive oil**

Place the beetroot in a medium saucepan and add the water, verjuice, chardonnay vinegar, saffron, sugar, salt and freshly ground pepper. Poach gently, uncovered, for 2 hours or until the beetroot are tender. Remove from the heat and allow to cool slightly in the poaching liquor. When cool enough to handle, peel the beetroot.

Pour the poaching liquor through a fine sieve lined with muslin cloth. Bring the strained liquor to the boil, lower the heat and reduce to a syrup. Remove from the heat and allow to cool.

Beat the goat's cheese and crème fraîche together in a bowl until smooth. Stir in the shallots and fresh herbs. Season to taste with salt and freshly ground pepper.

Slice the beetroot and then chop as fine as possible. Add 5 ml of the reduced cooking liquor to the chopped beetroot and season to taste with salt and freshly ground pepper.

Place an 8 cm diameter pastry ring in the centre of a plate, spoon the chopped beetroot into it and smooth with the back of the spoon. Gently remove the pastry ring. Place a tablespoon-sized quenelle of the goat's cheese mixture in the centre of the beetroot. Garnish with a few leaves of baby beetroot and sorrel and drizzle with the reduced beetroot syrup and olive oil.

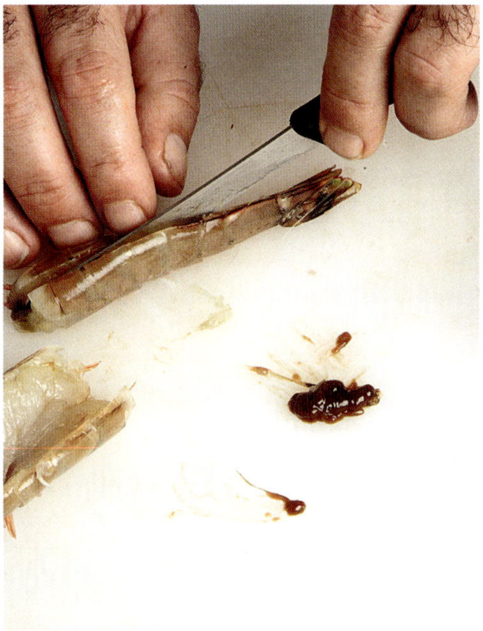

SHELLFISH

BASIC TECHNIQUE 1

Preparing and Cleaning Fresh Prawns

Prawns are probably the most widespread and popular crustacean of all. They live in both cold and warm water and are available all year round.

Of the cold-water variety, Dublin Bay prawns (also known as langoustine or scampi) are the finest and most expensive. They should only be bought live and frisky as they are often trawled in deep water, processed and quickly frozen. Once defrosted, they can become mushy and hard to peel and are best avoided.

Of the warm-water variety, look for Giant or Black Tiger prawns, Banana prawns, King prawns or Endeavor prawns. A lot of these are trawled and kept in an ice-cold sea water slurry to keep them fresh and are mostly sold in the shell.

When choosing prawns it is preferable to buy them alive or at least fresh in the shell. The best prawns are firm, plump and translucent, with protruding eyes and feel heavy in relation to their size. Avoid prawns that are discoloured or whose eyes have collapsed – these are signs of either defrosting or old age. Prawns have a very short shelf life and deteriorate rapidly once dead. Since they do not tolerate changes in temperature or too much exposure to the air, they should be peeled, have the intestinal vein removed and then should be stored between two damp cloths in the fridge until ready to use.

To shell and clean prawns, twist and pull the prawn heads from the bodies. Gently squeeze the shell of the prawn body to loosen it before peeling the shell from the base of the head to the tail.

Prawns have a dark intestinal vein running the length of their bodies that must be removed before cooking. Using the tip of a sharp paring or filleting knife, make an incision down the back of each prawn, from the base of the head to the tip of the tail, exposing the intestinal tract. Open up the prawn and remove the tract with the tip of a knife.

Rinse the prawn heads and shells under cold running water and reserve, as they are both full of flavour. Use for Shellfish Stock (*Basic Recipe 7, page 19*), bisques, sauces, flavoured butters and Crustacean Oil (*Basic Recipe 28, page 68*). Prawns can be substituted with lobster, crayfish, marron, scampi or yabbies.

Prawns in Potato Waistcoats with Curry Salt

Serves 4

	vegetable oil for deep-frying
12	**large potatoes, thinly sliced lengthways**
12	**prawns, peeled and deveined, with tail on (*Basic Technique 1, page 89*)**
	sea salt
	freshly ground pepper
	cornflour, mixed to a thick paste with cold water
	curry powder
4	**lemon wedges**

Heat the vegetable oil in a heavy-based saucepan over medium heat to 110 °C. Add the potato slices and sauté without colour until they are almost cooked.

Remove from the oil with a slotted spoon, taking care not to break them. Lay the slices on a tray lined with greaseproof paper, with a space between each one so they do not touch each other. Set aside until ready to use.

Lightly season the prawns with salt and freshly ground pepper. Lay a potato slice on a clean work surface and brush the edges with the cornflour paste. Place a prawn tail at one end of the potato and roll the potato tightly around it. Repeat with a second slice of potato so the prawn is covered, leaving only the tail exposed. Secure the potato with a small cocktail stick. Prepare the remaining prawns in the same way. Refrigerate until ready to cook.

Mix equal quantities of sea salt and curry powder together in a bowl.

Return the oil to the heat and heat to 180 °C. Arrange the prawns on a slotted spoon and carefully lower into the oil. Cook the prawns in batches until the potatoes are crisp and golden brown in colour.

Using a slotted spoon, carefully remove the prawns from the oil and place them on kitchen paper to absorb any excess oil. Lightly season the prawns with curry salt and serve immediately with a wedge of lemon.

Escabèche of Prawn and Scallop with Citrus Salad

Serves 4

Scallops have a rounded, ribbed shell and vary in size from the Small Bay scallop or Queen scallop, to the larger, plump, sweet, King scallop.

When buying scallop meat you really need to buy it from a reputable fishmonger as some processors pump scallops with water to plump them up. When cooked, they release all this water and end up boiling in their own juices, losing the colour, flavour and texture they once had. Avoid frozen scallop meat at all costs as half their weight will be water.

The best time to buy fresh scallops is during the winter months and early spring when they have large roes; the rest of the year the roe is virtually non-existent. Whenever possible, buy King Diver scallops that have been hand-picked from the ocean bed. They are very expensive but ensure ultimate freshness. Their shells should be tightly closed. To open them, insert a long, thin-bladed knife into the hinge and run it along the roof of the scallop to cut through the mussel that holds both shells together. Separate the shells and, using a tablespoon, gently detach the scallop from the shell. Remove the coral and black skirt and lay the scallop meat on a clean tea towel to absorb any moisture. The coral can be dried and ground into a powder and used as a seasoning or added to butter to use for finishing fish sauces.

Scallop flesh is very gelatinous and can absorb a lot of liquid, which makes it good for making delicate mousse. Or, simply slice and marinate scallops in a little citrus juice, olive oil and spices. Take care not to mask scallops with big flavours as they are very sweet and delicate.

20 ml	**extra virgin olive oil**
8	**fresh scallops, muscles removed**
8	**green prawns, peeled, deveined and halved lengthways (*Basic Technique 1, page 89*)**
	salt
	freshly ground pepper
8	**pink grapefruit segments**
8	**orange segments**
8	**lime segments**
8	**asparagus spears, peeled, blanched and sliced (*Basic Technique 17, page 184*)**
40 g	**large Tomato Concassée (*Basic Technique 13, page 177*)**
24	**mache leaves (lamb's lettuce)**
12	**sprigs fresh chervil**

Prepare the escabèche first. Place the coriander seeds, shallots, fennel, zests, orange juice, Pernod, white wine vinegar, olive oil and saffron threads into a heavy-based saucepan. Bring to the boil, reduce the heat and cook for 7–10 minutes, or until the vegetables are tender. Allow the escabèche to cool for 15 minutes.

Heat the olive oil in a heavy-based pan and sear the scallops and prawns for 15 seconds, ensuring that they remain undercooked.

Drain and lay the shellfish in a deep tray. Lightly season with salt and freshly ground pepper and allow to cool. Pour the escabèche over the shellfish and refrigerate for at least 30 minutes but no more than 3 hours to allow the flavours to infuse.

Lift the shellfish out of the escabèche and dry on a clean tea towel. Arrange the shellfish in a bowl plate and reserve the escabèche for dressing.

Mix the citrus segments, asparagus and tomato concassée in a bowl, lightly season with salt and freshly ground pepper and spoon over and around the shellfish. If necessary, add more olive oil to slightly thicken the escabèche and drizzle it over and around the shellfish. Garnish with the mache leaves and chervil.

Escabèche

5 ml	coriander seeds, crushed
2	shallots, finely sliced
1	bulb baby fennel, thinly sliced
	zest of ½ lemon
	zest and juice of ½ orange
15 ml	Pernod
45 ml	white wine vinegar
45 ml	olive oil
	pinch saffron threads

BASIC TECHNIQUE 2

Cooking and Preparing Crayfish

Crayfish must be purchased alive because enzymes in the tomalley (digestive gland) begin breaking down the meat within hours of death. In general, crustaceans are highly perishable, spoiling within hours of harvest. When buying live crustaceans, especially crayfish, check to ensure they are lively. They should have a clean, fresh scent and no ammonia odour, which indicates deterioration.

Preparing live crayfish for the first time can be daunting, but there are humane ways of preparing them without causing distress to the creature. Place the crayfish in a freezer compartment for 2 hours before cooking – this will cause it to sleep and hibernate. Remove it from the freezer and firmly insert the tip of a sharp knife through the centre of its head. This will kill the crayfish instantly without causing pain.

Crayfish taste best when cooked in the shell, as the shell releases some of its flavour into the meat and also protects the meat from losing flavour.

Bring a Court-Bouillon (*Basic Recipe 9, page 21*) or water to the boil in a heavy-based saucepan, then reduce the heat to a simmer. Lower the crayfish into the court-bouillon and cook for 7–9 minutes, depending on their size. Remove the saucepan from the heat and allow the crayfish to cool in the court-bouillon.

When cold, remove the crayfish from the court-bouillon and prepare the crayfish meat. Hold the crayfish firmly behind the head. Grip the middle of the tail with your thumb and forefinger, twist the body and pull away from the head. Using a heavy, sharp knife, split the head lengthways in half. Remove and discard the gritty sac from behind the eyes. Remove any meat from inside the head and reserve. Remove the green tomalley (the 'liver') and the coral (roe); both of these can be added to sauces to enhance flavour. Rinse the head under cold running water. Using kitchen scissors, cut along the underside of the crayfish on both sides, taking care not to cut into the meat. Gently pull the tail meat away from the shell, keeping it in one piece.

Crayfish have a dark intestinal vein running the full length of their bodies that must be removed before cooking. Using the tip of a sharp paring or filleting knife, make an incision down the back of each crayfish, from the base of the head to the tip of the tail, exposing the intestinal tract. Open up the crayfish and remove the tract with the tip of a knife. Lay the cleaned crayfish between damp cloths and refrigerate until ready to use.

If not using the shells for presentation, rinse the crayfish heads and shells under cold running water and reserve for Shellfish Stock (*Basic Recipe 7, page 19*), bisques, sauces, flavoured butters and Crustacean Oil (*Basic Recipe 28, page 68*).

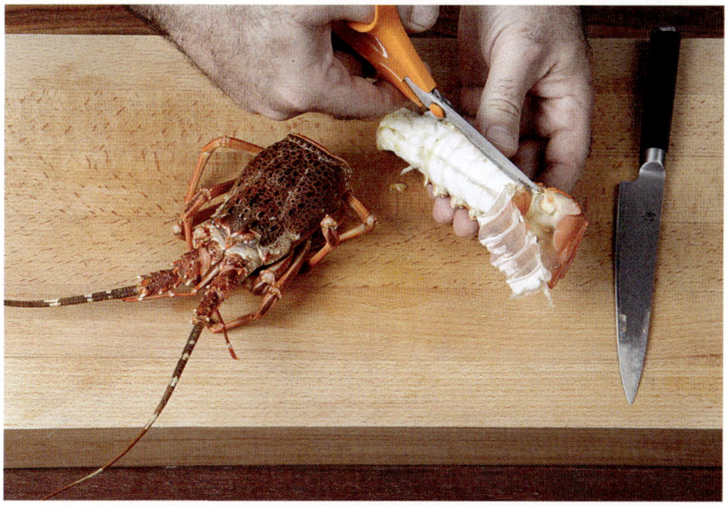

Poached Crayfish Tail with Mango and Basil Dressing

Serves 4

I am not a big fan of pairing fruit with savoury dishes, with a few exceptions such as venison and figs, game fowl with citrus fruits and this mango dressing with crayfish or prawns. For best results the mango must be fully ripened and sweet. Use a peppery extra virgin olive oil and a good-quality sherry vinegar or verjuice for the dressing. Make the dressing about an hour before serving and keep refrigerated until you are ready to dress the crayfish.

2 L	**Court-Bouillon (*Basic Recipe 9, page 21*)**
4	**live crayfish, about 350 g each (*Basic Technique 2, page 94*)**
1	**ripe mango**
8	**fresh basil leaves**
65 ml	**extra virgin olive oil**
	sherry vinegar or verjuice
	salt
	freshly ground white pepper
¼	**English cucumber**
8	**sprigs fresh basil**

Bring the court-bouillon to the boil in a heavy-based saucepan, reduce the heat and simmer for 30 minutes. Lower the crayfish into the court-bouillon and cook for 7–9 minutes, depending on their size. Remove the saucepan from the heat and allow the crayfish to cool in the court-bouillon.

When cold, remove from the court-bouillon and prepare the crayfish meat. Hold the crayfish firmly behind the head. Grip the middle of the tail with your thumb and forefinger, twist the body and pull away from the head. With a heavy, sharp knife split the head lengthways in half. Remove and discard the gritty sac from behind the eyes. Remove any meat from inside the head and reserve. Remove the green tomalley (the 'liver') and the coral (roe). Rinse the head under cold running water. Using kitchen scissors, cut along the underside of the crayfish on both sides, taking care not to cut into the meat. Gently pull the tail meat away from the shell, keeping it in one piece. Using the tip of a sharp paring or filleting knife, make an incision down the back of each crayfish, from the base of the head to the tip of the tail, exposing the intestinal tract. Open up the crayfish and remove the tract with the tip of a knife. Using the scissors, cut the tail shell in half lengthways.

Cut a cheek off the side of the mango and reserve for garnish. Peel the remaining mango and remove all of the flesh from the stone. Place in a food processor and blend to a purée. With the motor running, add the basil leaves and olive oil and blend until fully incorporated. Add sherry vinegar or verjuice to taste. Lightly season the dressing with salt and freshly ground white pepper. Refrigerate until ready to use.

Remove the reserved mango from its skin and slice thinly. Cut the cucumber into julienne. Chop the meat from the head of the crayfish. Gently mix together the chopped crayfish meat, half of the sliced mango and all the cucumber in a bowl and bind with a little dressing. Season to taste with salt and freshly ground white pepper. Spoon the mix into the shell of the head and set on a chilled plate. Slice the crayfish tail into 6 even medallions. Lightly coat them in a little dressing and arrange them into half a shell. Set beside the head, arranging the crayfish in its original form. Spoon a little more dressing over the crayfish and garnish with the remaining sliced mango and sprigs of basil. Serve the remaining dressing separately.

To maximise its flavour the crayfish should be served at room temperature, dressed in the chilled dressing.

Cooking and Picking Fresh Crab

Buy live crabs as the flesh deteriorates very quickly once they are dead. Fresh crab is also easier to clean and pick and will give a larger yield of meat. Check that both claws and all the legs are still attached to the body. The crab should feel heavy in relation to its size.

Preparing live crab for the first time can be daunting, but there are humane ways of preparing them without causing distress to the creature. Place the crab in a freezer compartment for 2 hours before cooking – this will cause it to sleep and hibernate.

Bring a large saucepan of water to the boil and add 150 g salt to every 5 litres. Reduce the heat to a simmer and plunge the crab into the water. A mud crab weighing between 800 g and 1 kg will take 9 minutes to cook and will yield approximately 45 per cent of its body weight in crab meat. Remove the crab from the water and cover with a cold damp cloth. Refrigerate to cool while it continues to steam in its own juices. Allow the meat to set. Set a small metal bowl into a larger bowl half-filled with ice. The smaller bowl will catch the crab meat as it is picked and will ensure that it remains chilled.

To extract the cold crab meat, begin by breaking down the crab into pieces. Remove both claws and the legs from the body and set aside. Firmly hold the crab and use your thumb to remove the shell from the body of the crab. Remove the stomach sac and gills ('dead man's fingers') from the body and discard, leaving just the body of the crab. Cut the body in half horizontally with a heavy knife. This will allow easier access to the meat. Using a skewer, pick out the meat from the cavities of the body.

Place the claws inside a clean tea towel and gently crack the shells with the back of a heavy knife or a mallet. Take care not to crush the meat. Peel away the shell to expose the meat. Repeat this process with all the legs until the entire shell is removed.

Pick through the crab meat with your fingertips once more to ensure that no fragments of shell remain. Refrigerate until ready to use.

BASIC TECHNIQUE 4

Shucking Oysters

Select live oysters with the shells firmly closed and avoid pre-shucked specimens at all costs. To open the oysters, a specially designed oyster knife is required. The oysters should be opened only at the last minute before serving.

Place the oyster onto a damp cloth, cupped side down. This is the side of the shell that holds the oyster meat and juice. Fold the cloth over the top of the oyster to hold it steady and to protect your hand from the shell.

Insert the tip of the oyster knife between the joint of the two shells, at the narrow end of the oyster. Put some pressure on the knife and gently twist the blade until the two shells separate. Take care not to push the tip of the blade too far in, to avoid puncturing the oyster. Gently pull the lid off the oyster and use the tip of the knife to separate the oyster from the muscle that attaches it to the lid.

When shucked, discard the lid and place the oyster into an empty egg carton to keep the oyster upright and prevent the juice from spilling out of the oyster shell.

Freshly Shucked Oysters with Chorizo and Shallot Vinaigrette

Serves 4

100 ml	**Red Wine and Shallot Vinaigrette (*Basic Recipe 32, page 72*)**
5 ml	**olive oil**
40 g	**chorizo, finely diced**
1	**small bunch fresh chives, finely sliced**
	salt
	freshly ground pepper
12	**unshucked oysters**
4	**lemon cheeks**

Pour the red wine and shallot dressing into a bowl. Heat the olive oil in a heavy-based pan over medium heat. Add the diced chorizo and cook, tossing frequently until it releases some of its fats. Transfer the chorizo directly from the pan into the red wine and shallot dressing and stir through. Add the chives and stir through the dressing. Taste and adjust the seasoning if necessary.

Shuck the oysters (*Basic Technique 4, page 100*). Arrange three small mounds of rock salt or crushed ice on each plate and place an oyster on top of each one.

Spoon the dressing over the oysters. Garnish with a cheek of lemon.

Oyster Beignets

Makes 12

125 g	**plain flour, sifted**
30 ml	**cold water**
110 ml	**beer, heated slightly until warm**
30 ml	**olive oil**
1	**free-range egg yolk**
	vegetable oil for deep-frying
2	**free-range egg whites**
	extra plain flour, sifted, for dusting oysters
	salt
	freshly ground pepper
12	**unshucked oysters (*Basic Technique 4, page 100*)**
	Maldon sea salt
	lemon juice

Prepare the first stage of the batter for the beignets: Whisk together the flour, cold water, warm beer, olive oil and egg yolk to form a smooth batter. Scrape down the sides of the bowl and cover with clingfilm to prevent a skin forming. Allow the batter to stand at room temperature for 1 hour.

Shuck the oysters (*Basic Technique 4, page 100*) and remove from the shells. (Reserve the juices for making Vichyssoise of Oysters, *page 33*.)

Heat the vegetable oil to 180 °C. In a clean bowl, whisk the egg whites until they form peaks and then fold through the batter mixture. Lightly season the extra flour with salt and freshly ground pepper. Dust the oysters with the flour, place them into the batter, and gently work with your fingertips until each oyster is evenly coated. Remove the oysters from the batter, allowing any excess batter to drain off. Place into the oil and cook until the batter puffs up and becomes crisp. Turn the oysters with a fork and continue to cook until golden. Using a slotted spoon, remove the oysters from the oil and drain on kitchen paper. Lightly season the beignets with Maldon sea salt, freshly ground pepper and a squeeze of fresh lemon juice.

Serve with Vichyssoise of Oysters (*page 33*).

GUINNESS

Freshly Shucked Oysters with Bloody Mary Jelly

Serves 4

A lovely entrée for a Sunday brunch. The jelly is prepared in the same way as Tomato and Basil Consommé (*page 28*) but with the addition of different ingredients and flavourings. Prepare the jelly in advance and open the oysters at the last moment (*Basic Technique 4, page 100*). Set the oyster shells in salt or on crushed ice, spoon the jelly over them and garnish with diced tomato, celery and cucumber.

500 g	**overripe vine-ripened tomatoes**
1	**shallot, peeled and sliced**
1	**stick celery, sliced**
1	**small bunch fresh basil, roughly chopped**
10 ml	**vodka**
	pinch Maldon sea salt
	pinch sugar
	pinch cayenne pepper
	Worcestershire sauce
	Tabasco sauce
1½	**sheets gelatine, soaked in cold water**
12	**unshucked oysters**
40 g	**Tomato Concassée (*Basic Technique 13, page 177*)**
40 g	**diced celery**
40 g	**diced cucumber**
	salt
	freshly ground pepper
12	**celery leaves**

Core the tomatoes and roughly chop. Place in a bowl with the sliced shallot, celery, basil, vodka, sea salt, sugar and the cayenne pepper. Mix the ingredients together and cover with clingfilm. Refrigerate for 4 hours to allow the flavours to infuse. After 4 hours, transfer the contents of the bowl into a double layer of muslin cloth and tie it up as tightly as possible. Place in a sieve over a large bowl to catch all the juice released from the tomatoes. Return to the fridge for 12 hours.

After 12 hours the tomatoes will have released all their juice and the sediment will have sunk to the bottom of the bowl. Using coffee filter paper, carefully decant the juice into a clean bowl, taking care not to disturb the sediment on the bottom. Discard the sediment and tomato pulp. Add Worcestershire sauce and Tabasco sauce to the juice to taste, and another dash of vodka if necessary.

Soften the gelatine in cold water. Squeeze the gelatine and dissolve in 25 ml of the tomato juice. Stir it into the remaining juice and set in the fridge. When the jelly has set, break it up with a fork.

Shuck the oysters (*Basic Technique 4, page 100*). Arrange three small mounds of rock salt or crushed ice on each plate and place an oyster on top of each one. Spoon the jelly over the oysters. Mix the tomato concassée, celery and cucumber together in a bowl and season with salt and freshly ground pepper. Spoon the vegetables over the jelly and garnish with a celery leaf.

BASIC TECHNIQUE 5

Preparing and Cleaning Mussels

The mussels found for sale are a cultivated variety. Wild mussels can be gathered from seashores everywhere, but these do tend to be small and quite leathery, as well as being susceptible to contamination, rendering them dangerous for consumption.

It is important to choose only the freshest live mussels with their shells tightly closed. Mussels can be kept alive for a few days before cleaning and cooking by keeping them covered with a damp newspaper or tea towel in the fridge.

As with most shellfish, mussels should be checked to ensure that they are still alive. Place the mussels in a colander under cold running water and give them a good shake – any mussels that remain open should be discarded. If a mussel feels heavy for its size, it is a sign that it is full of mud or sand and should also be discarded.

When preparing mussels, scallops and clams, bear in mind that they are always full of sand and therefore cannot be washed too often. With both mussels and clams, allow them to sit in clear water for 15 minutes, having first checked that they are alive, then change the water, allow them to sit for another 15 minutes, and repeat the process one more time.

Just before cooking, mussels should be debearded and scraped with the back of a knife to remove any barnacles.

Moules Marinière

Serves 4

In France, Belgium and the Netherlands, moules marinière is typically served with French fries or sliced baguette and a good beer.

25 ml	**olive oil**
1	**onion, peeled and finely chopped**
3	**cloves garlic, peeled and finely chopped**
3	**large sprigs fresh thyme**
2 kg	**fresh mussels**
250 ml	**white wine**
150 ml	**fresh cream (optional)**
1	**small bunch flat-leaf parsley, finely chopped**
	salt
	freshly ground pepper
1	**lemon**

Scrub and debeard the mussels. Rinse them under cold running water to remove any sand and grit. Discard any broken or open mussels (*Basic Technique 5, see above*).

Heat the olive oil in a heavy-based saucepan over medium heat. Add the onion, garlic and thyme and sweat for 2–3 minutes without colour. Add the mussels and stir for 1 minute. Add the white wine, cover the saucepan with a tight-fitting lid and bring back to the boil. Cook for 3–4 minutes until the mussels open, taking care not to overcook them. Add the cream and bring to the boil, then reduce the heat to medium and cook for a further 2 minutes.

Remove from the heat and tip the mussels into a colander placed in a bowl to catch all of the sauce. Return the sauce to the heat and add the chopped parsley. Season to taste with salt, freshly ground pepper and a squeeze of fresh lemon juice.

Divide the mussels between 4 warm serving bowls and pour the sauce over.

home made

FISH

Fish is exceptionally versatile and diverse, with each species having its own particular texture and flavour. People are often unsure of what to do with fish or, more importantly, uncertain of what to look for when buying it. Although it can be difficult to obtain fresh fish and shellfish, the first lesson is to find a reputable fishmonger or outlet that sells fresh, whole fish. Fish are seasonal and you should be guided by your fishmonger – he or she is the expert.

The most important part of your fish dish is to choose the freshest fish possible. Frozen fish should not be used and neither should tinned, bottled or preserved, where possible.

The first thing to look for when buying fresh fish is the eyes, as they will tell you a lot about the age and quality. Fresh fish have bright, clear, protruding eyes. Next check the gills – they should be bright red. The skin should have a sheen to it and the scales should be tight and firmly attached to the skin.

Fish are firm when they are first caught. When choosing a whole fish, gently press the flesh with the tip of your finger. The flesh should bounce back to its original shape. If it feels soft or spongy or the flesh is dull, these are signs that it is past its best.

If buying filleted fish the signs of freshness are harder to detect. The flesh should be firm and translucent and should have a pleasant smell. If it smells unpleasant and strong it should be avoided, so too if the flesh is loose and ragged.

Preparing fish is probably what puts many people off buying it as a whole piece. If you don't feel like preparing it yourself, ask your fishmonger to prepare it in the way you need it for your recipe. Ask for the head and bones for preparing fish stock.

Cooking Fish

When cooking fish, keep the preparation as simple as possible. Season the fish lightly before cooking to prevent the salt from drawing out the juices and season again lightly after cooking to obtain maximum flavour. If cooking whole fish, make diagonal slits with a sharp knife on either side so that the heat penetrates the fish evenly.

POACHING

Cover the fish with a court-bouillon or flavoured stock and cook over the lowest heat possible; the stock should barely tremble. On no account should the stock boil as it will result in a tough, overcooked piece of fish. When the fish is three-quarters cooked, remove it from the heat and allow it to finish cooking in the stock. Remove the fish and reduce the stock to concentrate the flavour and serve with the fish.

STEAMING

Place the fish on a perforated rack or in a Chinese steam basket over a pot of simmering water until the fish is opaque. When the fish is three-quarters cooked, switch off the heat and allow it to finish cooking in its own residual heat.

BAKING

This cooking method is more suited to whole fish. Season the fish lightly and place in a baking tray greased with butter or olive oil to prevent it from sticking. Scatter diced shallots and fresh herbs over the tray to add flavour. Pour some stock or white wine over and around the fish to create moisture to prevent the fish from drying out. Baste the fish with the liquid regularly as it cooks. Alternatively, follow the same method as described, but seal the fish in aluminium foil – this keeps the fish moist as it cooks in its own juices.

'EN PAPILLOTE'

Tightly seal seasoned pieces of fish in buttered greaseproof paper with the addition of thinly sliced vegetables, herbs and spices with a dash of wine or flavoured stock. As the fish cooks the steam generated causes the paper to puff up. Serve the package sealed so your guests can open the parcel themselves and appreciate the wonderful aromas that will billow out, adding a little theatre.

GRILLING

This cooking method is suitable for small whole fish or fish steaks such as tuna or swordfish. Heat the grill in advance. When grilling whole fish, use a sharp knife to make diagonal slits on both sides so that the heat penetrates the fish evenly. Lightly oil and season the fish on both sides or marinate it for 2–3 hours before cooking.

SHALLOW-FRYING

To shallow-fry fish, use a mixture of half oil and half butter and heat in a heavy-based pan over medium heat until the butter is foaming. Add the fish and cook until the flesh is caramelised before turning and cooking the opposite side. Baste the fish with the oil and butter mixture as it cooks. Avoid turning the fish repeatedly otherwise it won't caramelise. Towards the end of cooking, add a squeeze of fresh lemon juice to the pan and lightly season with salt and freshly ground pepper.

DEEP-FRYING

Fish needs a protective coat of seasoned flour, batter or breadcrumbs before it can be deep-fried. The fish being fried should be of even thickness to ensure that it is cooked evenly throughout. Use clean vegetable oil and heat it to 190 °C before submerging the fish into it. Do not add too much fish at the same time as the oil temperature will drop, preventing the outside of the fish from sealing and allowing the oil to penetrate the fish. If cooking several pieces of fish, allow the oil to come back to temperature before adding the next batch. When the fish is cooked, drain it on kitchen paper to absorb any excess oil and lightly season with salt and freshly ground pepper. Allow the oil to go cold before passing it through a fine sieve to use again.

BASIC TECHNIQUE 6

Filleting a Whole Salmon

Great care must be taken when handling fresh fish, particularly if it is going to be eaten raw. Work in a clean area with clean knives and cutting boards and keep the fish well chilled at all times.

Salmon is one of the most beautiful and versatile fish available and salmon farming accounts for most of the salmon consumed today. There are numerous ways of preparing salmon: raw as sashimi or tartare, smoked, marinated, confit, poached, grilled, pan-fried, or turned into mousse or brandade. Cook salmon skin-side down in the pan, turning it over three-quarters of the way through cooking, keeping the centre pink.

A glossy, smooth skin, bright red gills, protruding eyes and firm flesh indicate the freshness of a salmon. Choose salmon between 2.5 and 3 kg in weight, which will yield 8–10 portions.

The scales of the salmon must be removed before cooking as they are inedible and impossible to cut through with a table knife. Do this when the fish is whole before filleting it. It is a good idea to do this with the fish on a large plastic refuge bag, as the scales fly in all different directions. Hold the fish by the tail with a damp cloth so that you have a firm grip and, using the back of a knife, at a slight angle, scrape from the tail to the head to remove all the scales. Rinse the whole fish under cold water and pat dry with a cloth before filleting or cutting into darns.

Trim the fins with kitchen scissors as they can be very sharp and give a nasty cut. Cut the gills away as they will impart a bitter flavour if left on the fish during cooking. Lay the fish on its side and cut through to the bone at an angle just behind the gills. Keep the edge of the blade at a slight angle against the bone and continue cutting in an even stroke towards the tail until the fillet is free. Turn the fish over and repeat on the opposite side.

If a recipe calls for the skin to be removed, lay the fillet skin-side down on a chopping board. Make an incision through the flesh at the tail end. Hold the skin tightly in your hand. Work the knife from side to side between the flesh and skin, working the knife towards the opposite end and at the same time pulling the skin with the other hand. Remove the bloodline.

Using a pair of pliers or fish tweezers, remove the small line of pin bones that run down the centre of the flesh, from the head to two-thirds of the way down the fillet. Run your fingers or the back of a knife down the fillet to make the bones easier to find.

Once filleted, trim up the fillet neatly, removing the thin belly flap. Save the salmon bones and head for making stock that can be flavoured and reduced to make a savoury jelly or can be clarified to make a consommé. The fish is now ready to be portioned and cooked.

Picture on next page

Marinated Salmon with Crab and Lime Crème Fraîche

Serves 4

400 g	fresh salmon fillet
25 g	Maldon sea salt
10	coriander seeds
10	white peppercorns
10 ml	sugar
	zest and juice of 1 lime
100 g	picked crab meat (*Basic Technique 3, page 98*)
20 ml	crème fraîche
	salt
	freshly ground pepper
60 g	brunoise of peeled and seeded cucumber
60 g	brunoise of red onion
60 g	brunoise of peeled red pepper
60 g	brunoise of blanched and seeded tomato
5 ml	extra virgin olive oil
48	picked chervil leaves

Remove the skin, bloodline and pin bones from the salmon (*Basic Technique 6, page 111*). Place the sea salt, coriander seeds and peppercorns in a pestle and mortar and crush to a coarse powder. Add the sugar, lime zest and juice and mix together. Evenly spread the marinade over the salmon. Wrap the salmon in clingfilm and refrigerate for 6 hours. Wipe off the marinade with a damp cloth and dry the salmon on a clean tea towel.

Bind the crab meat with the crème fraîche in a bowl. Season to taste with salt, freshly ground pepper and a squeeze of lime juice. Slice the marinated salmon thinly and arrange on chilled plates, using an 11 cm pastry ring to create neat rounds. In a bowl, mix the cucumber, red onion, red pepper and tomato with the extra virgin olive oil and lightly season with salt and freshly ground pepper. Spoon the vegetables over the entire surface of the salmon.

Shape the crab meat between 2 tablespoons to form a quenelle and place in the centre of the salmon. Garnish with the picked chervil and drizzle a border of extra virgin olive oil around the salmon.

Gravlax with Mustard and Dill Dressing

Serves 12–16

It is very difficult to make gravlax with a small piece of fish and is better made with a whole side of salmon. It needs 30 hours to marinate and will keep in the fridge for up to a week if it is kept covered. Open the salmon every day and baste it with its juices (the salt will keep drawing moisture from the fish) to keep it moist. Other fish such as mackerel, trout and herring can be prepared in the same way but will need less curing time as they are smaller.

650 g	**side of fresh salmon, trimmed and pin boned (*Basic Technique 6, page 111*)**
12	**white peppercorns, coarsely crushed**
50 g	**Maldon sea salt**
4	**juniper berries**
50 g	**sugar**
60 g	**fresh dill**
	juice of 1 lemon

Mustard and Dill Dressing

1	**free-range egg yolk**
10 ml	**Dijon mustard**
	pinch sugar
150 ml	**vegetable oil**
	salt
	freshly ground pepper
	lemon juice
30 ml	**chopped dill**

Mix the peppercorns, sea salt, juniper berries and sugar together. Pick the dill from the stalks and refrigerate half of it until ready to use. Roughly chop the remaining dill and the stalks together.

Spread a sheet of aluminium foil large enough to wrap the salmon on your work surface. Cover the aluminium foil with clingfilm. Place the salmon, flesh-side up, onto the clingfilm. Evenly spread the salmon with the salt and sugar mixture. Squeeze the juice from the lemon over the fish and spread the dill over the salt and sugar. Wrap the fish tightly in the clingfilm and again in the aluminium foil. Place the salmon parcel on a tray and refrigerate for 24 hours.

After 24 hours open the parcel and, using the back of a knife, gently scrape the fish clean, saving all the juice for basting the fish. Spoon the juice over the fish. Finely chop the reserved dill and spread an even layer over the entire fillet. Wrap the fish once more and refrigerate for a further 6 hours.

To make the mustard and dill dressing, whisk the egg yolk, mustard and sugar together in a bowl until light and airy. Gradually whisk in the oil until fully incorporated, as if making mayonnaise. If the sauce becomes too thick, add a few drops of warm water to thin it out. Season the dressing with salt, freshly ground pepper, lemon juice and a pinch of sugar. Add the dill to the dressing just before serving to prevent it from discolouring.

Carve thin slices of salmon the same thickness as you would for smoked salmon. Arrange the slices on a chilled plate and serve with the dressing and either a small green salad or a potato salad dressed in extra virgin olive oil.

Picture on next page

Miso Salmon

Serves 4

Miso Salmon

600 g	**fresh skinless salmon fillet (*Basic Technique 6, page 111*)**
5 ml	**miso paste**
30 ml	**vegetable oil**
1	**shallot, peeled and finely chopped**
2.5 cm	**piece fresh ginger, peeled and finely chopped**
	salt
75 g	**fresh breadcrumbs**
2	**spring onions, finely sliced**
1	**free-range egg white**
15 ml	**soy sauce**
5 ml	**light sesame oil**
2.5 ml	**mustard seeds**
5 ml	**sesame seeds**

Glaze

7.5 ml	**miso paste**
30 ml	**Sugar Syrup (*Basic Recipe 53, page 229*)**
5 ml	**soy sauce**

In a small bowl, mix together the ingredients for the glaze and set aside.

Place 350 g of the salmon in a food processor with 5 ml of miso paste and blend to a fine paste. Dice the remaining salmon. Chill separately in the refrigerator for 20 minutes.

Heat 15 ml vegetable oil in a small pan, add the shallot and ginger and sweat without colour until softened. Remove from the pan and allow to cool.

Remove the processed and diced salmon from the fridge and place in the same bowl. Add the shallot and ginger, and a pinch of salt and mix together.

Add the remaining ingredients, except the sesame seeds, and bring the mix together. Shape into 4 even-sized rounds and refrigerate until ready to use.

Heat the remaining vegetable oil in a non-stick frying pan over medium heat. Cook the salmon on both sides until golden brown – 3–4 minutes per side – brushing them regularly with the glaze as they cook.

Remove from the pan and place one on each of 4 plates. Sprinkle each one with sesame seeds. Arrange a small pile of salad and dressing of your choice on top of each salmon and drizzle the dressing over and around the salad.

Salmon Confit

Makes 2 x 350 g screw-top jars

400 g	**fresh salmon, trimmed of all fat and sinew (*Basic Technique 6, page 111*)**
1 cm	**piece fresh ginger**
6	**white peppercorns**
5 ml	**coriander seeds**
5 ml	**Maldon sea salt**
2	**slices lemon**
1	**dried bay leaf, split in half**
2	**sprigs fresh thyme**
4	**slices red chilli with seeds**
250 ml	**extra virgin olive oil**

Preheat the oven to 120 °C. Cut the salmon into large, even-sized chunks. Peel the ginger and slice into 4 pieces. Crush the peppercorns and coriander seeds. Arrange the salmon chunks on a tray and evenly season with salt, crushed peppercorns and crushed coriander seeds.

Divide the salmon between the jars and add the ginger, lemon, bay leaf, thyme and sliced chilli. Fill the jars with the extra virgin olive oil, put the lid on and screw it tight.

Cook in a bain-marie for 1 hour. Remove from the oven and allow to cool at room temperature. Once cold, keep refrigerated until ready to use.

Picture on page 108

BASIC TECHNIQUE 7

Filleting Sole

Sole has always been considered one of the best flat fish, its flesh being firm, white and delicate of flavour. After standing for a day or two, the flesh of sole improves due to a chemical reaction within the enzymes in the fish. Skinning a sole is easy, as the skin will just pull away from the flesh, but this cannot be said of all soles – lemon sole will not do this, but nevertheless is a fine substitute for sole.

Lay the sole on a clean chopping board with its head away from you. With the tip of a sharp filleting knife, make an incision through the skin 5 mm from the base of the tail. Holding the tail firmly, pull away the skin, from the tail to the head. The skin should come away in a single piece. Turn the fish over and repeat with the other side.

Trim off the fins using kitchen scissors. With the tip of the knife, scrape away any blood at the back of the head and remove any roe. Using a heavy knife, remove the head. Rinse the cavity of the fish under cold running water and pat dry with a clean tea towel.

Place the fish back on the chopping board. With the tip of the knife, make an incision down the centre of the fish from the head to the tail. Keep the edge of the blade at a slight angle against the bone and continue cutting in even strokes towards the tail until the fillet is free. Remove the top two fillets from the fish, turn the fish over and repeat on the opposite side.

Once filleted, trim up the fillet neatly. Save the bones for making stock. The fish is now ready to be portioned and cooked.

POACHING SOLE

Lightly season each fillet with salt and freshly ground pepper. Roll up each fillet neatly, starting from the tail end, and secure each one with a cocktail stick.

Lightly butter a heavy-based saucepan and add a chopped shallot and sprigs of thyme. Place the fillets on top and pour in a little fish stock or water and white wine. Cover with buttered greaseproof paper and gently poach over a low heat for 5–6 minutes, depending on the thickness of the fillets. Remove the fillets and keep warm while you prepare the rest of the dish.

GRILLING SOLE

Grilling flat fish such as sole, lemon sole and plaice on the bone retains the flavour of the fish and keeps the flesh succulent. Buy fresh sole on the bone and remove the skin, head and the fin bones from the side of the fillet.

Heat a grill plate over a high heat. Season the sole with salt and freshly ground pepper and lightly dust with flour, shaking off any excess. Lightly oil the grill plate with a little oil soaked into a clean cloth. Cook the fish on the grill plate for 3–4 minutes per side, turning the fish at a 90° angle after 2 minutes to achieve lattice grill marks.

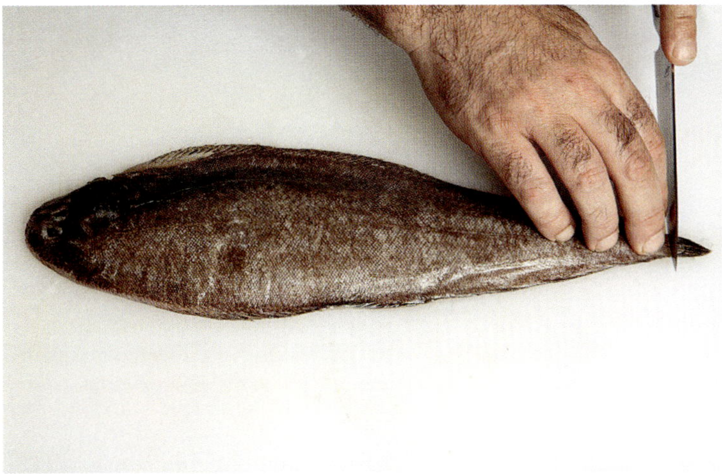

Sole à la Meuniere

Serves 4

4	**sole, skin removed and cleaned (*Basic Technique 7, page 120*)**
	seasoned flour for dusting
25 ml	**olive oil**
100 g	**unsalted butter**
50 ml	**white wine**
	juice of 1 lemon
25 ml	**Veal Jus (optional) (*Basic Recipe 11, page 41*)**
1	**small bunch flat-leaf parsley, finely chopped**
15 g	**salted capers (optional)**
	salt
	freshly ground pepper

Lightly dust the sole in the seasoned flour. Heat the olive oil in a frying pan large enough to hold the 4 sole over medium heat. Place the sole into the pan and cook until golden brown. Carefully turn the fish over and cook the other side until golden brown. Remove the sole from the pan and keep warm while you make the sauce.

Return the pan to the heat and add the butter. Cook over medium heat until the butter melts and becomes nut-brown in colour. Add the white wine and lemon juice and cook for 30 seconds. Add the veal jus and cook for 30 seconds. Add the chopped parsley and capers. Remove from the heat and season to taste with salt and freshly ground pepper.

Serve the fish whole or debone the fish and arrange 4 fillets in the centre of each of 4 warmed plates. Spoon the sauce over the fish and serve immediately.

Poached Sole with Crustacean Oil

Serves 4

4	**sole (350 g each), skin removed and filleted (*Basic Technique 7, page 120*)**
	salt
	freshly ground pepper
50 g	**unsalted butter**
1	**shallot, peeled and finely diced**
4	**sprigs fresh thyme**
300 ml	**Fish Stock (*Basic Recipe 6, page 17*)**
100 ml	**white wine**
8	**green asparagus spears, peeled and blanched (*Basic Technique 17, page 184*)**
150 ml	**Crustacean Oil (*Basic Recipe 28, page 68*)**
100 g	**shrimps, peeled**
2	**shallots, peeled and finely sliced**
1	**branch fresh thyme, leaves picked**
200 g	**Tomato Concassée (*Basic Technique 13, page 177*)**
15 ml	**sliced chives**
15 ml	**finely chopped flat-leaf parsley**
1	**lemon**
12	**sprigs fresh chervil**

Lightly season each fillet with salt and freshly ground pepper. Roll up each fillet neatly, starting from the tail end, and secure each one with a cocktail stick.

Lightly butter a heavy-based saucepan and add the chopped shallot and sprigs of thyme. Place the fillets on top of the shallot and thyme and pour in the fish stock and white wine. Cover with buttered greaseproof paper and poach for 5–6 minutes, depending on the thickness of the fillets. Remove the fillets and keep warm while you prepare the rest of the dish.

Cut the tips off the asparagus spears and slice the stems at an angle into 3 cm pieces.

In a saucepan, warm 100 ml crustacean oil, add the shrimps and sauté until golden brown. Add the shallots, asparagus and thyme, reduce the heat and continue to cook until the shallots have softened. Add the remaining crustacean oil, tomato concassée, chives and parsley. Season to taste with salt, freshly ground pepper and a squeeze of fresh lemon juice.

Remove the fillets from the poaching liquid and drain on a clean tea towel. Place each sole in the centre of 4 warmed plates and spoon the garnish around it in neat piles. Spoon the crustacean oil from the pan over and around the sole. Garnish with sprigs of chervil.

Seared Tuna or Tataki of Tuna

Serves 4

Seared Herbed Tuna

600 g tail piece of tuna, skin and sinew removed
5 ml chopped tarragon
5 ml chopped flat-leaf parsley
5 ml chopped chervil
5 ml sliced chives
salt
freshly ground pepper
25 ml olive oil
20 ml Dijon mustard
1 lemon

Prepare the tuna several hours before serving: Using a long, thin-bladed knife, trim the tuna into a neat 400 g cylinder. Tightly wrap in several layers of clingfilm and refrigerate until ready to use. Use the trimmings of the tuna for another dish such as Tartare of Tuna (*page 129*).

Mix together the tarragon, parsley, chervil and chives in a bowl and spread out on a small tray. Unwrap the cylinder of tuna and lightly season with salt and freshly ground pepper. Heat the olive oil in a non-stick pan until almost smoking. Add the tuna and quickly and evenly sear it, keeping it rare inside. Remove the tuna from the pan and allow to cool before brushing with a thin layer of mustard. Roll the tuna in the herb mixture so that the entire piece is coated. Roll the herbed tuna in several layers of clingfilm and refrigerate while preparing the remainder of the chosen dish.

Slice the tuna into 4 neat medallions using a sharp knife. Carefully remove the clingfilm. Brush each slice with extra virgin olive oil and lightly season with salt, freshly ground pepper and a squeeze of lemon. Serve with a garnish of your choice.

Seared Peppered Tuna

10 g white peppercorns
10 g black peppercorns
10 g pink peppercorns
10 g green peppercorns
25 ml extra virgin olive oil

Prepare the tuna as described in the recipe above. Unwrap the cylinder of tuna and lightly season with salt and freshly ground pepper. Heat the olive oil in a non-stick pan until almost smoking. Add the tuna and quickly and evenly sear it, keeping it rare inside. Remove the tuna from the pan and allow to cool.

Place the peppercorns in a food processor and blend to a powder. Add the olive oil to bind the peppers together to form a paste. Roll the tuna in the paste until evenly coated and roll tightly in several layers of clingfilm. Refrigerate overnight to allow the pepper flavour to penetrate the tuna.

Seared Tuna with Wasabi and Sesame Seeds

20 ml wasabi paste
30 ml toasted sesame seeds

Prepare the tuna as described in the recipe above. Unwrap the cylinder of tuna and lightly season with salt and freshly ground pepper. Heat the olive oil in a non-stick pan until almost smoking. Add the tuna and quickly and evenly sear it, keeping it rare inside. Remove the tuna from the pan and allow to cool.

Once cold, brush the tuna with the wasabi paste and roll it in the sesame seeds so that the entire piece is coated. Roll the tuna in several layers of clingfilm and refrigerate until ready to use.

Seared Tuna with Soba Noodles

Serves 4

600 g	tail piece of tuna, skin and sinew removed
10 ml	peanut oil
20 ml	wasabi paste
30 ml	toasted sesame seeds
100 ml	Japanese mayonnaise
	wasabi paste
200 g	dried soba noodles
2	spring onions, julienned
5 ml	poppy seeds
	salt
	freshly ground pepper
1	sheet nori
15 ml	light sesame oil
1	lemon

Prepare the tuna several hours before serving: Using a long, thin-bladed knife, trim the tuna into a neat 400 g cylinder. Tightly wrap in several layers of clingfilm and refrigerate until ready to use. Use the trimmings of the tuna for another dish such as Tartare of Tuna (*page 129*) or Grilled Skewers of Tuna (*page 130*).

Unwrap the cylinder of tuna. Heat the peanut oil in a non-stick pan over medium heat until almost smoking. Add the tuna and quickly and evenly sear it, keeping it rare inside. Remove the tuna from the pan and allow to cool. Once cold, brush the tuna with the wasabi paste and roll it in the sesame seeds so that the entire piece is coated. Wrap the tuna in several layers of clingfilm and refrigerate while preparing the remainder of the dish.

Mix the Japanese mayonnaise and wasabi paste to taste and set aside.

Bring a large pot of lightly salted water to the boil. Add the soba noodles and cook until al dente (4–5 minutes). Drain the noodles in a colander and rinse under plenty of cold running water. At first the water will be milky, as the noodles will give off excess surface starch. Place the noodles into a bowl of iced water. When cold, remove them by hand, squeezing the noodles gently to shed any excess water. Transfer them to a bowl and dress with the wasabi mayonnaise. Add the spring onions and poppy seeds. Season to taste with salt and freshly ground pepper.

Slice the nori into a fine julienne using a sharp knife.

Unwrap the seared tuna and slice into 4 neat medallions using a sharp knife. Brush each slice with the sesame oil and lightly season with salt, freshly ground pepper and a squeeze of lemon.

Divide the noodles between 4 chilled plates, place a slice of tuna on top and garnish with the nori.

Tartare of Tuna with Togarashi Dressing

Serves 4

Whatever ingredient you are serving as tartare, it must be extremely fresh and well trimmed of all fat and sinew. It must also be kept chilled throughout preparation. This tuna tartare embraces Japanese flavours. If you can get wasabi tobiko (flying fish roe infused with wasabi) serve it with this dish as it adds a wonderfully crunchy texture. Allow your guests to add the salt and lime juice to their tartare; adding these beforehand will leach out the juices from the tuna. The tuna can be replaced with salmon, mackerel or swordfish.

Togarashi Dressing

10 ml **peeled and grated fresh ginger**
5 ml **finely chopped garlic**
2 **red chillies, seeded and chopped**
22.5 ml **light sesame oil**
30 ml **peanut oil**
juice of 1 lime
22.5 ml **soy sauce**
5 ml **sugar**
10 ml **hot chilli powder**

Tartare of Tuna

600 g **fresh tuna, trimmed and chilled**
1 **avocado**
¼ **English cucumber, diced**
pinch poppy seeds
pinch white sesame seeds
4 **lime wedges**

Place all of the dressing ingredients in a bowl and whisk together. Taste and adjust the seasoning if necessary. Refrigerate until ready to use.

Using a very sharp knife, dice the tuna – do not chop it or the texture will be ruined. Peel the avocado, remove the stone and slice the flesh into 1 cm slices.

Place a ring mould in the centre of each of 4 chilled bowl plates. Line the base of the mould with the avocado slices. Spoon the diced raw tuna onto the avocado to fill the ring, pressing it down gently with the back of the spoon to prevent it from falling apart once the mould is removed.

Carefully remove the mould. Spoon a little dressing over and around the tuna tartare. Spoon the cucumber over the tuna and then sprinkle with poppy seeds and sesame seeds. Serve with a lime wedge and the remaining dressing on the side.

Grilled Skewers of Tuna with Cucumber, Ginger and Chilli Salad

Serves 6

Cucumber has a mild flavour and high water content, making it a very refreshing vegetable to serve with Thai, Indian and Middle Eastern foods to temper the heat. With the addition of sugar, ginger and rice wine vinegar, this slightly sweet salad is great as a light entrée with a piece of grilled fish such as tuna or swordfish. Prepare the fish 8 hours in advance to allow the flavour of the lemon grass to penetrate the fish.

6	**stems lemon grass**
900 g	**fresh tuna fillet**
10 ml	**light sesame oil**
10 ml	**peanut oil**
	salt
	freshly ground pepper
	Cucumber, Ginger and Chilli Salad (*page 80*)
6	**lime wedges**

Peel the outer layers of the lemon grass to leave 6 thin sticks. Trim the tuna and cut into 18 even-sized cubes. Skewer 3 pieces of tuna onto each stick of lemon grass and arrange on a tray. Chop up the outer leaves of lemon grass and scatter over the tuna. Mix the two oils together and pour over the tuna, cover with clingfilm and refrigerate for 8 hours.

To serve, heat a grill plate over high heat. Drain the tuna from the marinade and lightly season with salt and freshly ground pepper. Brush with the oil from the tray. Cook the tuna on the grill plate for 2 minutes on each side, turning the fish at a 90° angle to achieve lattice grill marks. Keep the tuna medium-rare as it will start to dry out if cooked longer.

Spoon the cucumber salad into the centre of each plate and set a skewer of grilled tuna on top. Garnish with a wedge of fresh lime.

Tuna Confit

Makes 2 x 350 g screw-top jars

A simple and tasty way to prepare excess tuna. Delicious flaked through a tomato salad, mixed with mayonnaise and spring onion on toast or flaked over pasta with Parmesan cheese.

400 g	**fresh tuna, trimmed of all fat and sinew**
1 cm	**piece fresh ginger**
6	**white peppercorns**
5 ml	**coriander seeds**
5 ml	**Maldon sea salt**
2	**slices lemon**
1	**dried bay leaf, split in half**
2	**sprigs fresh thyme**
4	**slices red chilli with seeds**
250 ml	**extra virgin olive oil**

Preheat the oven to 120 °C. Cut the tuna into large, even-sized chunks. Peel the ginger and slice into 4 pieces. Crush the peppercorns and coriander seeds. Arrange the tuna chunks on a tray and evenly season with sea salt, crushed peppercorns and crushed coriander seeds.

Divide the tuna between the jars, and add the ginger, lemon, bay leaf, thyme and sliced chilli. Fill the jars with the extra virgin olive oil, put the lids on and screw tight.

Cook in a bain-marie for 1 hour. Remove from the oven and allow to cool at room temperature. Once cold, keep refrigerated until ready to use.

Tuna Niçoise

Serves 4

12	small potatoes
100 ml	basil pesto
	salt
	freshly ground pepper
1	lemon
6	marinated anchovy fillets
12	pieces semi-dried tomatoes (*Basic Technique 14, page 177*)
6	quail eggs, boiled for 2 minutes, refreshed and peeled
50 g	tapenade
150 ml	Beurre Blanc (optional) (*Basic Recipe 22, page 50*)
4	tuna portions (140 g each), seared and herbed (*Basic Technique 8, page 124*) or grilled
25 ml	extra virgin olive oil
80 g	French beans, topped, tailed and blanched
30 g	olives, sliced
12	leaves flat-leaf parsley
12	baby basil leaves

Preheat the oven to 140 °C. Heat a grill plate over high heat. Scrub the potatoes under cold running water and cook in salted water for 20 minutes, or until tender. Peel the potatoes while still hot and place in a bowl. Crush the potatoes with a fork and add pesto to taste (also colouring the potatoes a deep green). Season to taste with salt, freshly ground pepper and a squeeze of lemon. Cover with clingfilm and keep warm while preparing the remainder of the dish.

Halve the anchovies and lay a piece inside each of the semi-dried tomatoes. Fold over the tomatoes to enclose the anchovy, exposing the skin side of the tomato.

Halve the quail eggs and lightly season with salt and freshly ground pepper. Warm the quail eggs and semi-dried tomatoes in the oven.

If serving with tapenade beurre blanc, whisk the tapenade into the beurre blanc to taste, colouring the sauce charcoal. Check the seasoning and adjust if necessary with salt, freshly ground pepper and a squeeze of lemon.

If serving the tuna seared and herbed, slice the tuna into 4 even-sized pieces and brush with olive oil. Lightly season each slice with salt and freshly ground pepper.

If serving the tuna grilled, season the tuna with salt and freshly ground pepper and brush with extra virgin olive oil. Cook the tuna on the grill plate for 2–3 minutes on each side, turning the fish at a 90° angle to achieve lattice grill marks. Keep the tuna medium-rare as it will start to dry out if cooked longer.

Reheat the French beans in boiling salted water, drain and season to taste with salt, freshly ground pepper and a drizzle of extra virgin olive oil. Place a ring mould into the centre of each of 4 warmed plates and spoon the beans into the mould. Spoon a quarter of the pesto potato on top of the beans, pressing it down with the back of the spoon so that it is evenly and tightly packed together. Gently remove the mould and set 3 pieces of semi-dried tomato and 3 halves of quail egg around the potato. Spoon the olive slices around the plate. Spoon the tapenade beurre blanc over and around the garnish or drizzle with olive oil.

Lift the fish from the grill, brush with extra virgin olive oil, season with a squeeze of lemon and set on top of the potatoes. Garnish with the flat-leaf parsley and baby basil leaves.

MEAT AND POULTRY

When choosing meat and poultry, avoid vacuum-packed, preportioned meat from the supermarket shelves. Instead, buy it from a reputable butcher. There are many good reasons to patronise a dedicated, traditional butcher who focusses on quality rather than quantity. Your butcher should be able to tell you all about the meat you buy and the source of the food chain – how it was fed, how it was aged and how long it was hung for – and will also be able to source the unusual for you, such as pig's caul or fresh pig's blood. They also make their own small goods from scratch and, above all, they will sell you good, flavoursome meat.

The term 'poultry' applies to all types of domesticated fowl, whether they are bred for the table or for eggs. There are over 12 000 species of edible birds, but the most commonly served are generic farmyard birds, notably chicken, duck, goose, guinea fowl and turkey.

Game can be divided into two categories: 'ground and winged' or 'feathered and furred'. Game meat can be either wild or farmed, but is now farmed in ever-increasing numbers and reared all the year round specifically for consumption. The popularity of game is on the rise as it is regarded as a healthy red meat, low in fat, calories and cholesterol, and a good source of protein and iron.

Beef benefits from being hung in cold storage for lengthy periods of up to, and over, forty days. This is done to develop its flavour and increase tenderness and a good butcher will automatically do this. During this time, natural enzymes in the meat break down connective tissues and fibres, making the flesh more tender. The meat will lose a lot of moisture, which results in loss of weight. Taking this into consideration, and that a pure breed will have excessive fat, dictates the higher price for a good piece of meat. Well-hung meat will have a dry, dull and dark outer layer surrounding it and the fat will have a yellow tinge to it, but once the meat is cut it will reveal a rich red colour and will have a good marbling of fat running through it – all signs of a quality and flavoursome piece of meat. Only the best grades of beef are dry-aged as the process is expensive.

Most meat is 'wet-aged' (in Cryovac packs) for 7–28 days. The same enzymes are still breaking down the same proteins, but because it occurs in a sealed, wet environment, the meat stays very juicy. Wet-aged meat doesn't have the same depth of flavour as dry-aged meat and often has a metallic flavour to it.

Veal is the meat of an unweaned calf of 110–120 days old. It is not the most popular of meats due to the cruel way in which it is still reared in some countries. It is possible, however, to find veal that has grazed on the pastures and been suckled until slaughter. Veal is a very versatile meat with many cuts particularly good for roasting, braising and poaching. The bones and feet from veal are very gelatinous and produce a superior stock that is used as the base for many sauces.

Sweetbreads come from two different areas of the calf: the thymus gland located in the throat and the pancreas or 'heartbreads' located near the stomach, which are larger, meatier and have less fat and gristle surrounding them than the thymus gland. Sweetbreads should be soaked under cold running water to remove any trace of blood before being briefly blanched in a Court-Bouillon (*Basic Recipe 9, page 21*) to firm them slightly and preserve their colour, also making it easier to peel the thin layer of skin that surrounds them.

Veal tongue should also be rinsed under cold running water and the roots from the tongue should be removed. Poach the tongue in water or chicken stock with mirepoix for 3 hours, or until the thick skin covering the tongue peels away easily. Once the skin has been removed the tongue should be sliced thinly lengthways before being served either hot or cold (see *page 150*).

The livers and kidneys from calves have a very delicate flavour and a smoother texture than that of ox or pig's liver. The kidneys are encased in a thick layer of suet that should be rendered down and used as lard or in suet pastry for pies.

Most pork on the market has been reared indoors and fed on meal, which results in very lean animals. Pork is best bought from a specialist pork butcher, who will sell an outdoor-reared breed of pork such as the Saddleback or Tamworth, which will be fatter, meatier and have more flavour than the alternatives. It will also be able to provide fresh charcuterie, sausages, pancetta, pig's blood, caul, ears, head, skin for crackling and feet.

The whole head of the pig has many tasty bits and is full of flavour. Braise slowly in stock until the meat falls off the bone. Allow the head to cool before removing the tongue, cheeks and ears. Reduce the braising stock by half, skimming regularly. Once reduced, pass it through a fine sieve and let it set into jelly. Peel the thick outer skin and remove the roots from the tongue. The meat from the head and tongue can be shredded and stirred through the jelly with some chopped parsley to make brawn. The pig's ears can also be cut into thin strips, double-crumbed and fried until crisp in clarified butter.

The pig's caul is a web-like sheet of fatty membrane that surrounds the intestine of the pig. It has a very strong smell and needs to be rinsed under cold running water until the water runs clear and all traces of blood are gone. Squeeze the caul dry before wrapping around meats that benefit from being basted, as the caul renders down during cooking and seeps back into the meat, helping to keep it moist. It is also used to hold stuffing in place during cooking.

Offal, otherwise known as 'variety meats' or 'organ meats', covers the edible internal parts and some extremities of an animal, removed before the carcass is cut up. Some of the most flavoursome and tastiest cuts of the animal come from the head, snout, tail, tongue, ears, liver, stomach (tripe), kidneys, trotters, bone marrow, sweetbreads (pancreas and thymus glands), brains and giblets (the offal from poultry).

Cuts of Meat

When choosing meat it is important to know what cut you are buying in order to cook it correctly. There are two types of meat: tender and tough. Think of meat as a muscle and you'll soon appreciate why muscles that work harder (those in the leg and neck) make for chewier meat, full of connective tissue, gristle and collagen, while those along the back are soft and tender. Meat becomes more tender the further it is from the hoof or snout.

An animal is divided into four quarters: two big front pieces and two rear pieces. The forequarter sections yield cuts such as boneless shin, bone-in shin, cross rib roast, brisket and various cuts of chuck and blade, and the neck is sold as stewing steak or minced meat. Short ribs and flank are also cut from this section of the animal. The rear part of the forequarter yields fore rib and back rib roasts, and cuts that are called cube roll (scotch fillet) and standing rib roast. With the exception of the aforementioned cuts, the meat from this area is best suited for slow, moist methods of cookery, such as braising, stewing or pot-roasting.

The hindquarters yield a wide variety of cuts, including the most tender. Sirloin, tenderloin (eye fillet), rump, topside and silverside come from here, as do skirt steak, flank, oxtail and round steak from the knuckle region. Bone-in shin meat also comes from the hindquarters.

Charcuterie means 'cooked meat' and also describes a shop where such products are produced and sold. Charcuterie is predominantly made from pork, but poultry, feathered and furred game and offal are also used to make a variety of products using various types of preparations, such as salt curing, air drying and smoking. Charcuterie also includes dishes such as pâtés, terrines, sausages, rillettes, hams, crépinettes, blood sausage and boudin blanc.

Cooking and Preparation Techniques for Meat and Poultry

BARDING

To surround meat, poultry or game with pork fat to keep the meat moist while it cooks. Not to be confused with lard, which means to insert fat into meat, poultry or game for the same reason.

BASTING

To keep poultry, game, meat or fish moist and to add flavour during cooking, by spooning over the pan juices or fat.

BLANCHING

Some meats such as bacon are blanched to reduce their salt content. Others can be blanched in a simmering court-bouillon to seal them before pan-frying, such as calf's sweetbreads.

BRAISING AND STEWING

Braising is suited to either whole joints or smaller cuts of meat and poultry. The meat is sealed and evenly browned, and then covered with an appropriate flavoured stock, aromatic vegetables and seasonings. It is slowly cooked, covered with a lid in an oven at a low temperature, until tender. When cooked, the stock will have reduced to sauce consistency.

CONFIT – SEE *BASIC TECHNIQUE 12, PAGE 168*

GRILLING

Grilling is a wholesome, easy method of cooking where a heavy metal grate or solid grill plate is set over hot coals or another heat source. Top or bottom open heat is used to cook foods such as small to medium fish and shellfish, cuts of meat such as sirloin, T-bone, scotch fillet, rump or hamburgers, as well as poultry, game and various vegetables such as onions, aubergines, potatoes and asparagus. The term barbecue or braaiing is often used synonymously with grilling. The following points should be adhered to for a successful grill or braai: Only a small amount of oil should be used; too much oil will cause flames on the grill. To begin with, the grill should be between 220 and 260 °C to seal large cuts of meat and fish. It is then reduced to 150–200 °C towards the end of the cooking process. The higher temperature will seal the pores.

Most prime cuts of meat are sold pre-cut and packaged; they are often cut too thin for grilling, resulting in overcooked and dry meat. Ask your butcher to cut the meat at least 5–6 cm thick and, where possible, to keep it on the bone.

MARINATING – DRY AND WET

To soak food such as meat, fish or vegetables in a seasoned liquid, paste or dry rub called a marinade. The purpose of marinating is for food to absorb the flavour of the marinade or to tenderise meat.

PAN-FRYING/SHALLOW-FRYING

This method is good for medium-thick steaks, escalopes or minute steaks, hamburgers, sausages and meatballs. The meat is seared quickly on each side in a very hot pan to seal in the juices and form a crust, then the heat is reduced and the meat cooked to the required temperature. Rare meat has an internal temperature of 60 °C, medium 70 °C and well-done 75 °C. The longer meat is cooked, the dryer and tougher it becomes.

POACHING

A gentle, moist heat cooking method carried out in a liquid, flavoured stock, broth or in a container set in a bain-marie at 65–80 °C. Poaching is best suited to delicate foods such as fish, shellfish and poultry, as well as lean, prime cuts of meat such as beef fillet or lamb loin. It is also used to cook eggs and fresh fruits such as peaches or pears.

Food is gently cooked in liquid just below simmering point, when the surface is just showing some trembling movement. The amount and type of liquid used depends on the particular food and quantity being poached. Poaching produces a delicate flavour in foods while imparting some of the poaching liquid's flavour to the ingredient and vice versa.

Meats and poultry are usually poached in a flavoured stock such as chicken or beef, with the addition of aromatic vegetables and a bouquet garni, which is then reduced to concentrate the flavour and served with the meat. The reduced liquid can be transformed into a sauce with the addition of a thickening agent like cream, butter or a vegetable purée and flavoured with alcohol, herbs or spice.

POT-ROASTING

A process by which food is placed in a covered pan in the oven with mirepoix and a generous amount of butter at approximately 140–210 °C. Place the mirepoix in the pan with the meat or poultry and the butter. Cover the pan and cook slowly in the oven in its own juice at a low temperature, basting regularly. Just before the end of the cooking time, remove the lid and allow the meat to colour. Remove the meat and add some stock to the pan and reduce. Strain, skim and season to taste. Serve this with the meat.

RENDERING

The process of melting animal fat over low heat to separate it from skin, meat and bones. Rendered pork fat is known as lard (see *Basic Technique 12, page 168*).

RESTING

As meat cooks, particularly larger cuts or whole birds, the heat cooks the meat from the outside inwards, driving all the moisture from the meat to the centre. The heat also causes the fibres in the meat to tense so it is important to give it time to rest after cooking and before carving, so that the meat juices can redistribute through the meat evenly, allowing the fibres to relax, resulting in a tender piece of meat. The larger the piece of meat, the longer resting time should be allowed. The meat may need to be returned to the oven for a short period before serving to bring its temperature back up.

ROASTING

Roasting cooks food by surrounding it with dry heat, the same principle used for baking in the oven. It is an excellent way to cook meat, fish, poultry, vegetables and potatoes. Large joints of meat are generally cooked at high temperature to cook the surface and seal in the juices, and then the heat is reduced for the remaining cooking time. Before roasting, bring the food to room temperature to reduce the cooking time required.
If roasting a joint of meat that is uneven in shape, tie it with butcher's twine into a more uniform shape to ensure even cooking.

Place meat and poultry skin-side or fatty-side up to keep the meat or poultry moist during roasting. When roasting cuts of meat, poultry or fish with not much external fat, rub them with oil and baste them frequently while cooking. Place meat on a rack above a roasting tray to provide hot air circulation around the complete piece of meat and to catch any juices that run from it. Remove food 10 minutes before it is fully cooked through as it will continue to cook in its own residual heat once removed from the oven. Allow to rest before carving.

SAUTÉING

To cook food quickly over high heat in a small amount of fat, while moving the ingredients around in the pan.

SCORING

To make shallow incisions – 1 mm deep – in the skin or outer layer of ingredients before cooking, such as for fish and duck breasts. This assists in even cooking and prevents the food from shrivelling and becoming tough during cooking.

SEALING

To sear the surface of meat, poultry, game or fish in fat over a high heat in a pan or roasting tray to seal in moisture. Sear fish, poultry and feathered game skin-side down in the pan until crisp and golden brown.

SEARING

To cook very quickly over high heat.

SPATCHCOCKING OR BUTTERFLYING

A preparation that lends itself to cooking of young chickens. The backbone is removed and the breastbone flattened, allowing the bird to cook quicker.

BASIC TECHNIQUE 9

Trimming and Portioning Beef Fillet

The whole fillet or tenderloin is one of the choicest parts of the beef, not normally roasted whole but trimmed and cut into a variety of different cuts for different dishes.

The tail is either rolled and frozen for beef carpaccio (*page 144*) or sliced thinly for sautéed dishes such as beef stroganoff.

The head of the fillet and the thinner part of the tail are cut into small fillet mignon of 110–120 g or diced for steak tartare (*page 142*).

The centre of the fillet is cut into tournedos weighing 160–180 g or kept whole for beef wellington.

The thickest part of the fillet is used as chateaubriand of 600–650 g to serve 2.

To trim a whole beef fillet, start at the head of the fillet (the thickest part), cutting and lifting the fat from the meat. When the top layer of fat is loose, pull to separate it from the meat and trim it off as closely as you can to the meat.

Remove the chain, which is the long, thin piece of meat that is full of fat and runs down the full length of the side of the fillet. Trim and clean the chain and use it to make minced meat or sauces (*Basic Recipe 11, page 41*).

Pull the large lump of fat under the head of the fillet and sever it with your knife. Follow the natural line of the meat and remove the head. Remove all fat and silver skin from the head. Turn the fillet over and remove any excess fat from the underside.

Place the fillet back in its upright position. Pull the thin layer of fat to expose the large sinews and silver skin. Using a boning knife held at an angle, remove the sinews that cover the meat. Start from the top of the beef fillet and work towards the tail to remove all fat and sinew. Portion the fillet as required.

Picture on next page

Tartare of Beef

Serves 4

To retain maximum colour, texture and taste, do not dice and season the meat more than 20 minutes before serving. If prepared too far in advance, the meat will oxidise and discolour.

300 g	**beef fillet, cleaned of all sinew (*Basic Technique 9, page 139*)**
15 ml	**finely chopped gherkin**
15 ml	**finely chopped cocktail onions**
	rinsed and finely chopped capers to taste
15 ml	**sliced chives**
15 ml	**chopped flat-leaf parsley**
1	**large free-range egg yolk**
5–10 ml	**Dijon mustard to taste**
	dash Tabasco
	dash Worcestershire sauce
20 ml	**tomato ketchup**
	dash brandy
	salt
	freshly ground pepper
4	**free-range egg yolks for serving**

Set up a stainless steel bowl half-full of ice and place another bowl on top of the ice. Using a large, sharp chopping knife, dice the beef for the tartare very finely. Place the meat into the bowl and add the gherkins, cocktail onions, capers, sliced chives, chopped parsley and 1 egg yolk and mix through the beef. Add mustard, Tabasco, Worcestershire sauce, tomato ketchup and brandy to taste, depending on how spicy you want the tartare to be. Season to taste with salt and freshly ground pepper. Place the tartare in the fridge until you are ready to serve it.

Place a 6 cm ring mould in the centre of each of 4 plates and spoon in the tartare, pressing it down to form a smooth round. Place each remaining egg yolk back into a half shell and set in the centre of the tartare. Serve with toasted sourdough bread.

P
S

Carpaccio of Beef

Serves 4

The fillet of beef for the carpaccio must be prepared and rolled at least 12 hours in advance of serving as it needs to be frozen before it can be sliced.

300 g **beef fillet, cleaned of all sinew** (***Basic Technique 9, page 139***)
salt
freshly ground pepper

Wrap the beef in several layers of clingfilm and roll up tightly to form an even piece of meat. Place in the freezer, preferably overnight.

Remove the clingfilm from the frozen fillet of beef and slice the meat as thinly as possible on a slicing machine. If you don't have a slicing machine, place the beef in the freezer to firm up but don't let it freeze completely. Carve the beef into thin, even slices using a sharp knife. Lay each piece between 2 layers of clingfilm and place on a heavy chopping board. Use a meat mallet or a heavy rolling pin to beat the slices into large, wafer-thin pieces.

Spread overlapping slices of beef onto a chilled plate to cover the entire surface. Lightly season the carpaccio with salt and freshly ground pepper.

The carpaccio can be served with pesto, grated Parmesan cheese, rocket leaves and a wedge of lemon.

Beef Burgers or Meatballs

Serves 4

15 ml	olive oil
100 g	finely chopped onion
1	clove garlic, peeled and finely chopped
30 ml	brown sugar
	juice and zest of ½ lemon
800 g	good-quality, lean, coarsely minced beef, chilled
50 g	bone marrow, sliced
2.5 ml	ground cumin
2.5 ml	ground coriander
1 ml	Dijon mustard
15 ml	Worcestershire sauce
1	free-range egg yolk
15 ml	chopped basil
15 ml	chopped Italian parsley
	salt
	freshly ground pepper

Heat the olive oil in a heavy-based saucepan over medium heat. Sweat the onion and garlic for 2 minutes without colour. Stir in the sugar, lemon juice and zest and continue to cook until the sugar has dissolved. Remove from the heat and allow to go cold.

Place the chilled meat in a large bowl. Add the cold onion mix and remaining ingredients. Season with salt and freshly ground pepper and mix thoroughly. Refrigerate for 1 hour.

Using wet hands shape the mix into 4 even-sized burgers or into 24 meatballs.

Entrecôte Café de Paris

Serves 4

12	**slices (25 g each) Café de Paris Butter (*Basic Recipe 23, page 54*)**
4	**entrecôte steaks (260 g each)**
	olive oil
	salt
	freshly ground pepper

Remove the café de Paris butter from the freezer and place in the fridge for 2 hours before using to make it easier to slice.

Trim the steaks, leaving a good layer of fat on them. Heat a cast-iron grill plate over a medium heat. Turn the grill on to the highest setting.

Rub the steaks lightly with olive oil and place on the grill until sealed and well coloured on that side. Turn and cook the opposite side to your liking. Remove the steaks from the grill and allow to rest for 5 minutes before carving into 6 even slices. Season the meat with salt and freshly ground pepper. Place the steaks onto a tray and spread the slices of café de Paris over the entire surface of the steaks. Place under a hot grill until the butter melts and begins to gratinate. Transfer the steaks to warmed plates and serve immediately with French fries.

Confit Pork Belly

Serves 4

The texture of confit pork belly improves by brining it first before cooking, for anything from 24 hours to a week. To brine the pork belly, place the pork in a tight-fitting container and cover with cold water. Pour off the water and measure it. For every litre of water add 180 g salt. Pour the salted water into a heavy-based saucepan and place over medium heat until the salt has dissolved. Remove from the heat and set aside to go cold. Pour the brine over the pork belly and refrigerate for 24 hours to 1 week. Twenty-four hours before cooking, drain and dry the meat. Soak overnight in fresh water.

2 kg	**pork belly**
30 ml	**sea salt**
15 ml	**freshly ground pepper**
30 ml	**peanut oil**
200 ml	**soy sauce**
200 ml	**cold water**
50 g	**brown sugar**
2	**star anise**
2	**sticks cinnamon, broken up**
3 cm	**piece peeled fresh ginger, thinly sliced**
4	**cloves garlic, peeled and crushed**

Preheat the oven to 240 °C. Score the pork rind at 1 cm intervals. Place the pork into a deep, heavy-based roasting tray. Rub half of the salt, the ground pepper and peanut oil into the rind. Sprinkle the remaining salt over the pork. Roast for 20–30 minutes, or until the skin has crackled.

Remove the pork from the oven and add the soy sauce, the cold water, sugar, star anise, cinnamon, ginger and garlic to the tray. Reduce the oven temperature to 180 °C and cook for a further 70–80 minutes until the meat is tender. Carve and serve with garnish of your choice.

Braised Veal Shanks

Serves 4

4	baby veal shanks (300 g each)
	salt
	freshly ground pepper
250 ml	red wine
100 ml	port
25 ml	vegetable oil
100 g	carrot, peeled and chopped
100 g	onion, peeled and chopped
100 g	celery, sliced
4	cloves garlic, crushed
1 L	Veal Stock (*Basic Recipe 4, page 14*)
1	sprig fresh thyme
2	fresh bay leaves
1	sprig fresh rosemary

Preheat the oven to 140 °C. Lay the shanks on a work surface and season well with salt and freshly ground pepper.

Pour the red wine and port into a heavy-based saucepan and reduce by half over medium heat. Set aside until ready to use.

Heat the vegetable oil in a large cast-iron pan over medium heat. Add the veal shanks and render down the fat, turning them frequently for 15–20 minutes until they are nicely browned. As the fat renders down, pour it from the pan. It is important the pan retains its heat so as the shanks are evenly coloured and retain all their juices. Remove the veal shanks from the pan and return the pan to the heat. Add the chopped carrot, onion, celery and the crushed garlic and cook until golden brown. Pour the reduced red wine and port over the vegetables and deglaze the pan with it.

Transfer the vegetables and alcohol into a large heavy-based saucepan. Add the roasted shanks and cover with the veal stock. Return to the heat and bring to the boil. Reduce the heat so that the veal stock just simmers. It is important the cooking liquid just simmers during cooking to prevent the shanks becoming tough and chewy. Skim the surface to remove any scum that floats to the top. Add the thyme, bay leaves and rosemary to the saucepan, cover with a lid and transfer to the oven. Cook slowly for 3–4 hours, depending on the size of the shanks, until the shanks are tender and coming away from the bone. Carefully lift the shanks from the stock and place on a tray.

Reduce the remaining liquid to a sauce consistency until it is glossy and coats the back of a spoon. Season to taste with salt and freshly ground pepper. Pass through a fine sieve. Place the shanks back into the reduced sauce and gently warm through over a low heat.

Serve the shanks with Garlic Potato Purée (*page 217)* and Roasted Vegetables (*Basic Recipe 38, page 186*).

Poached Veal Tongue with Gribiche Vinaigrette

Serves 4

Veal Tongue

1	**veal tongue (620 g)**
1	**onion, chopped**
2	**carrots, chopped**
2	**sticks celery, chopped**
1	**small leek, chopped and washed in cold water**
2	**cloves garlic, crushed**
4 L	**Chicken Stock (*Basic Recipe 1, page 12)***
12	**white peppercorns, crushed**
2	**dried bay leaves**
2	**sprigs fresh thyme**
	selection of baby salad leaves
	flat-leaf parsley leaves

Gribiche Vinaigrette

40 ml	**freshly squeezed lemon juice**
	pinch sugar
110 ml	**extra virgin olive oil**
50 g	**gherkins, finely chopped**
50 g	**cocktail onions, finely chopped**
15 ml	**capers**
15 ml	**finely chopped mixed herbs (chives, flat-leaf parsley and tarragon)**
1	**hard-boiled free-range egg, sliced**
	salt
	freshly ground pepper

Preheat the oven to 140 °C. Soak the veal tongue under cold running water for 30 minutes. Drain the tongue and place in a large heavy-based saucepan with the onion, carrots, celery, leek and garlic. Cover with the chicken stock and gently bring to the boil. Reduce the heat and skim the stock well. Add the white peppercorns, bay leaves and thyme. Cover the pot with a lid and transfer to the oven to braise the meat slowly, barely simmering, for 2½–3 hours.

When the tongue is ready, the skin covering will peel away easily. If the meat requires additional cooking, simply return it to the oven and check again after a further 15 minutes. When the tongue is ready, remove the saucepan from the oven and allow to cool in the cooking stock.

Make the gribiche vinaigrette. Pour the lemon juice into a bowl and add a pinch of sugar. Whisk in the oil. Add the remaining ingredients and season to taste with salt and freshly ground pepper.

When the tongue is cold, lift it out of the stock. Peel the skin from the veal tongue. Pass the stock through a fine chinois and reserve for another dish.

Using a sharp carving knife or an electric slicing machine, slice the veal tongue lengthways into 16 slices, as thinly as possible. Brush both sides of the veal tongue with a little of the oil from the gribiche vinaigrette and lightly season with salt and freshly ground pepper. Lay 4 slices of the tongue on each of 4 plates, slightly overlapping each other. Arrange the salad leaves attractively over the tongue. Spoon a little more of the gribiche vinaigrette over and around the tongue and salad leaves and garnish with flat-leaf parsley.

Barbecue Pork

Makes 2 kg

2 kg	pork neck, cut into 4 cm strips

Marinade

4	spring onions, trimmed and roughly chopped
1	small bunch fresh coriander, stalks or roots only
2	shallots, peeled and roughly chopped
15	slices galangal
15	slices fresh ginger, skin on
375 ml	water
1	star anise
2 cm	piece cinnamon
2	cloves
	pinch five-spice powder
1	piece orange peel
60 ml	light soy sauce
15 ml	dark soy sauce
45 ml	Chinese rice wine
150 g	sugar

Basting Syrup

50 g	glucose
50 g	sugar
15 ml	light soy sauce
15 ml	honey
15 ml	hoisin sauce

To make the marinade, simmer the spring onions, coriander roots, shallots, galangal and ginger in the water in a heavy-based saucepan for 5 minutes. Dry-roast the star anise, cinnamon and cloves in a heavy-based pan until lightly toasted and aromatic. Add them to the stock, along with the five-spice powder and orange peel. Stir in the soy sauces, rice wine and sugar. Continue to simmer until the sugar has dissolved. Remove from the heat and allow to go cold.

Place the pork into a deep container and pour the cold marinade over, making sure the pork is completely immersed in the marinade. Refrigerate overnight.

Make the basting syrup by adding the glucose and sugar to 80 ml water in a heavy-based saucepan and simmering it until the sugar has dissolved. Stir in the soy sauce, honey and hoisin sauce, along with the cinnamon, star anise and cloves from the marinade. Continue to simmer for 3 minutes, then remove from the heat and transfer to a stainless steel bowl. Allow the syrup to go cold and thicken.

Preheat the oven to 140 °C. Remove the pork from the marinade. Lay the pork on a cooling rack set over a roasting tray. Roast the pork for 10 minutes before removing from the oven and brushing all over with the syrup. Increase the oven temperature to 180 °C. Return the pork to the oven and cook for a further 5 minutes. Baste the pork again and return to the oven for another 5 minutes. Baste the pork every few minutes, turning it over so it is evenly brushed and cooked. Remove from the oven and check if the pork is cooked (it must be well-done). When the pork is cooked, allow it to cool. Carve the pork into thin slices and serve in soups, stir-fries or on its own with steamed rice and a dipping sauce. The barbecued pork will keep for 3 days in the fridge.

Pork Crackling

Pork Crackling 1

300 g	**pork rind**
2.5 ml	**pimento**
1	**star anise**
2.5 ml	**ground nutmeg**
2.5 ml	**sweet paprika**
2.5 ml	**freshly ground pepper**
	zest and juice of 1 lemon
10 ml	**Maldon sea salt**

Using a sharp knife, remove any excess fat from under the pork rind. Dry-roast the pimento and star anise in a heavy-based pan and then grind with the nutmeg, paprika and pepper to a powder. Rub the ground spice, lemon and salt into the skin. Place on a tray, cover with clingfilm and refrigerate overnight. Cook in a low oven at 140 °C until crisp.

Pork Crackling 2

40 g	**pork rind**
	salt
5 ml	**vegetable oil**
	freshly ground pepper

Preheat the oven to 200 °C. Using a sharp knife, remove any excess fat from under the pork rind. Cut the rind into julienne, sprinkle with salt and allow to stand for 20 minutes to extract moisture from the rind – this will help to create crisp crackling.

Heat the vegetable oil in a heavy-based pan, add the pork rind and seal. Transfer the pan to the oven and cook for 10–15 minutes until crisp and golden, stirring occasionally. Remove the crackling from the pan and place onto kitchen paper to absorb any excess oil. Lightly season with salt and freshly ground pepper.

Baked Pork Ribs

Serves 4

15 ml	**vegetable oil**
16	**pork spareribs**
2	**spring onions, green part only, finely sliced**

Marinade

4	**shallots, peeled and finely chopped**
4	**cloves garlic, peeled and finely chopped**
	zest of ½ orange
30 ml	**brown sugar**
200 ml	**cider**
25 ml	**cider vinegar**
60 ml	**tomato ketchup**
60 ml	**HP sauce**
7.5 ml	**mustard powder**
15 ml	**clear honey**
2	**smoked chillies, finely chopped**
5 ml	**chilli powder or smoked paprika**
60 ml	**tomato paste**
40 ml	**Worcestershire sauce**
	salt
	freshly ground pepper

For the marinade, mix all of the ingredients together in a bowl. Season to taste with salt and freshly ground pepper.

Heat the vegetable oil in a large heavy-based frying pan over medium heat. Fry the ribs in batches for 2–3 minutes on each side until they are evenly coloured. Add more oil to the pan as necessary. Once browned, transfer the ribs to a large ovenproof dish.

Pour the marinade over the ribs and mix well to coat all over. Cover and refrigerate for 4 hours, turning the ribs occasionally.

Preheat the oven to 150 °C. Place the ribs in a single layer on a large baking tray and spoon the marinade over the ribs. Bake in the oven for 1 hour, turning and basting the ribs occasionally until they are tender and glazed, and the meat is just falling away from the bone.

Arrange on a serving platter and sprinkle with the spring onions.

Jointing a Chicken or any other Poultry or Game Bird

Rather than buying chicken pieces, buy a whole chicken and bone it yourself. The method below will result in 2 pieces each of wings, fillets, thighs, drumsticks and 4 pieces of breast, and you will be left with the carcass with which to make a fresh chicken stock (*Basic Recipe 1, page 12*).

All poultry and game birds have the same bone and carcass structure so once you master this technique you will be able to joint any bird.

Cut off the feet and neck. Remove the innards and separate the livers, gizzard and heart.

Pull the wing bone away from the breast and cut between the second joint, leaving the first section of the wing attached to the breast. Repeat with the second wing.

Pull a leg away from the body and, with the tip of a knife, cut through the skin to release the leg from the body. Bend the leg backwards until the ball of the thighbone pops out of the hip socket. Cut between this joint and keep the tip of the knife close to the carcass to remove the oyster so that it remains attached to the leg. Repeat with the second leg. Using the tip of your finger, feel for the joint between the thigh and drumstick. Cut firmly downwards to separate the two pieces.

To remove the breast, insert the tip of the knife into the neck end of the chicken. Twist the knife on its point, scraping it against the wishbone on both sides. Separate the wishbone from the flesh with your fingers and cut off the bone at the base, then pull it out. Run the tip of the knife along the backbone of the chicken. Keeping the tip of the knife against the carcass, follow the bone down and around the rib cage. Cut through the wing joint to release the breast from the carcass. Repeat with the other breast. Remove the fillet from each chicken breast. Cut each breast into 2 pieces.

To Tunnel Bone a Chicken Leg

Lay the chicken leg skin-side down on a clean chopping board. Using the tip of a boning knife, make an incision the length of the thighbone to reveal the bone. Scrape the tip of the knife down the bone towards the joint which holds the thigh and drum bones together, freeing the meat from the thighbone. Keeping the knife close to the joint, cut around it, taking care not to puncture the skin. Remove the joint and the thighbone. The drumstick bone will now be exposed. With the tip of the knife, scrape the meat from the drumstick bone until you can grip it. Pull the bone hard, holding onto the meat. This will turn the drumstick inside out and make removing the bone and sinew much easier. Slice across the piece of skin attached to the top of the drumstick to release the bone. Reverse the chicken leg so the skin is on the outside again. Reserve the bones for making chicken stock.

Coq au Vin

Serves 4

1	**whole free-range chicken (1.8 kg), jointed *(Basic Technique 10, page 156)***
100 g	**piece pancetta, cut into lardons**
	salt
	freshly ground pepper
40 ml	**olive oil**
10 ml	**sherry vinegar**
75 ml	**brandy**
75 ml	**port**
25 g	**butter**
20	**button onions or shallots, peeled**
20	**button mushrooms**
500 ml	**Veal Stock (*Basic Recipe 4, page 14*)**
15 ml	**chopped flat-leaf parsley**

Marinade

750 ml	**full-bodied, quality red wine**
4	**sprigs fresh thyme**
1	**dried bay leaf**
2	**sticks celery, chopped**
1	**large carrot, peeled and chopped**
1	**small onion, peeled and chopped**
4	**cloves garlic, peeled and crushed**

Make the marinade for the chicken: Put the red wine, thyme, bay leaf, celery, carrot, onion and garlic in a heavy-based saucepan and cook over medium heat until it has reduced by half. Remove from the stove and cool.

Place the chicken pieces and lardons in a large bowl and pour the red wine marinade over them. Move the chicken around with a spoon so it is all evenly coated with the red wine. Cover and marinate overnight in the fridge.

Strain the marinade and set aside. Set the lardons aside and discard the vegetables and herbs. Dry the chicken pieces on kitchen paper. Lightly season the chicken with salt and freshly ground pepper. Heat 25 ml of the olive oil in a heavy-based pan and seal the chicken pieces on both sides until evenly browned. Remove the chicken from the pan and place into a casserole dish. Pour off any excess oil from the pan and sauté the pancetta lardons until golden brown. Remove from the pan and set aside. Pour off any excess oil from the pan and deglaze with the sherry vinegar, brandy, port and the red wine marinade. Reduce by two-thirds, and then pour over the chicken pieces.

Melt the butter in a clean heavy-based pan and, when foaming, add the button onions. Cook until golden brown, season with salt and freshly ground pepper and drain in a sieve. Add the onions to the casserole. Sauté the button mushrooms in the remaining olive oil and season with salt and freshly ground pepper. When evenly browned, drain and reserve. Pour the veal stock into the casserole and bring to the boil. Reduce the heat and simmer for 20–25 minutes until the chicken is tender and cooked through, skimming frequently to remove the impurities that float to the surface.

Remove the chicken, lardons and button onions from the stock and pass the stock through a fine chinois into a clean pan. Bring to the boil and reduce until the sauce is syrupy and coats the back of a spoon. When ready to serve, return the chicken pieces to the sauce and add the lardons, onions, mushrooms and chopped parsley. Adjust the seasoning if necessary. Divide the coq au vin between warm serving plates. Serve accompanied by potato purée and braised baby carrots.

Chicken and Mushroom Pie

Serves 8

Poached Chicken

1	**whole free-range chicken**
2.5 L	**cold water or Chicken Stock (*Basic Recipe 1, page 12*)**
2	**onions, peeled and quartered**
2	**carrots, peeled and quartered**
2	**sticks celery, halved crossways**
½	**head garlic, peeled and halved crossways**
1	**dried bay leaf**
	salt
	freshly ground pepper

Sauce

30 g	**unsalted butter**
4	**shallots, peeled and finely sliced**
1	**clove garlic, peeled and finely sliced**
8	**button mushrooms, finely sliced**
2	**sprigs fresh thyme**
80 ml	**white wine**
200 ml	**Chicken Stock (*Basic Recipe 1, page 12*)**
350 ml	**fresh cream**
	salt
	freshly ground pepper
	dash Madeira wine

Garnish

50 g	**unsalted butter**
2	**leeks, white part only, sliced into 1 cm rounds**
	salt
	freshly ground pepper
100 ml	**Chicken Stock (*Basic Recipe 1, page 12*)**
75 ml	**olive oil**
200 g	**mixed mushrooms, trimmed and cleaned**
½	**bunch flat-leaf parsley, chopped**
½	**bunch tarragon, chopped**

1	**free-range egg yolk, whisked for egg wash**
8	**puff pastry discs, 3 mm thick, to overlap the rim of each pie dish by 1 cm**

Wash the chicken thoroughly under cold running water to remove any traces of blood. Remove the wings from the chicken and set aside for the sauce. Place the chicken into a heavy-based stockpot and cover with cold water or chicken stock. Add the onions, carrots, celery, garlic, bay leaf, salt and freshly ground pepper. Reduce the heat to a simmer and cook gently for 45 minutes. Do not boil the stock as the chicken will toughen. Switch the heat off and leave the chicken to rest in the stock for a further 15 minutes. Test a thigh with a skewer – if the juices run clear, the chicken is cooked. Allow the chicken to cool before removing and discarding the skin. Remove the chicken meat from the legs and breasts and break into large pieces. Set aside until ready to use.

Make the sauce. Heat the butter in a heavy-based pan over medium heat until just foaming. Add the shallots, garlic, mushrooms and thyme. Sweat for 5 minutes without colouring. Add the reserved chicken wings and continue to cook for a further 3 minutes. Pour in the white wine and continue to cook until it has evaporated completely. Add the chicken stock and cook until it has reduced by half. Add the cream and simmer for 10 minutes. Pass through a fine chinois. Season to taste with salt, freshly ground pepper and the Madeira. Set aside.

Prepare the garnish. Melt the butter in a heavy-based frying pan over low heat. Add the leeks, season with salt and freshly ground pepper and cook for 3–4 minutes until lightly coloured. Add the chicken stock and cook for a further 5 minutes until the leeks are three-quarters cooked, then set aside.

Heat the olive oil in a heavy-based frying pan over high heat. Add the mushrooms and sauté until golden brown. Season with salt and freshly ground pepper. Drain and set aside until ready to use.

Place the chicken, leeks, mushrooms and chopped herbs into a large bowl and mix together. Bind the chicken mixture with two-thirds of the sauce, then spoon into 8 individual pie dishes. Pour a little more sauce into each pie dish.

Brush the top of the inside of each dish with a little egg yolk, and then lay the pastry over the top, sealing it at the top edge and over the side of the dish. Slice off any excess pastry. Place the pies in the fridge for 30 minutes before baking.

Preheat the oven to 180 °C. Brush the pastry lids with egg wash and make 2 slits with the tip of a knife to allow the steam to escape. Bake for 25–30 minutes, or until the pastry is golden. Allow to rest a couple of minutes before serving. Serve with a side dish of Petit Pois à la Française (*Basic Recipe 44, page 195*).

BASIC TECHNIQUE 11

Preparing and Cooking Duck

Rather than buying duck portions, buy a whole duck and bone it yourself. Follow the instructions for jointing, *Basic Technique 10, page 156*, and use the carcass to make a fresh duck stock or a brown duck sauce, and any excess fat for rendering.

DUCK NECK

Using a boning knife, place the tip of the knife between the skin and the neck and carefully cut the skin, working from the top to the bottom and folding back the skin as you work the knife along the neck. Remove the skin in one piece without puncturing it. Turn the skin inside out and remove the windpipe and any excess fat from the skin. Remove the meat from the neck and use it, and the duck neck skins, for duck neck sausage filling *(page 175)*. Chop the neck into small pieces and use for stock or sauce.

DUCK LIVER

Fresh duck liver needs to be trimmed before using to remove any sinew and bile, a very bitter green fluid secreted by the liver and stored in the gall bladder. To rid the liver of bile, soak it in cold milk with a large bunch of fresh thyme and a sliced clove of garlic and refrigerate for a few hours. Drain and dry on a clean tea towel when ready to use. The liver will have absorbed the flavours of the garlic and thyme. Use the liver in stuffing or sear in clarified butter in a hot pan – keeping the centres pink; or transform into a smooth parfait with the addition of eggs and softened butter and flavour with reduced Madeira, port and cognac and cook in a terrine set in a bain-marie.

DUCK GIZZARD

The gizzard is a second stomach that the duck uses to grind up its food. It needs to be slit from top to bottom to reveal the inside, which is usually full of grain. Remove by peeling away the tough skin and sinew. Salt the gizzards for 3 hours and then slowly confit in duck fat for 2 hours until tender (*Basic Technique 12, page 168*). Allow to cool before thinly slicing and pan-frying in a little duck fat. Serve with salads or as a garnish with duck.

DUCK LEG

Like most poultry, the legs are tough and sinewy. They benefit from braising in a flavoured stock or cooking as confit (*Basic Technique 12, page 168*) rather than being roasted on the bird as they require longer cooking than the breasts.

DUCK BREAST

Roasting duck breasts on the bone contributes to the flavour. Remove the wishbone to make it easier to carve. Score the skin, taking care not to cut into the flesh, and seal on both sides in a heavy-based pan over medium heat for 4–6 minutes. The fat will render down and the skin will become crisp. Drain off and reserve the rendered fat. Use the carcass, wing bones and neck for stocks, sauces and consommé.

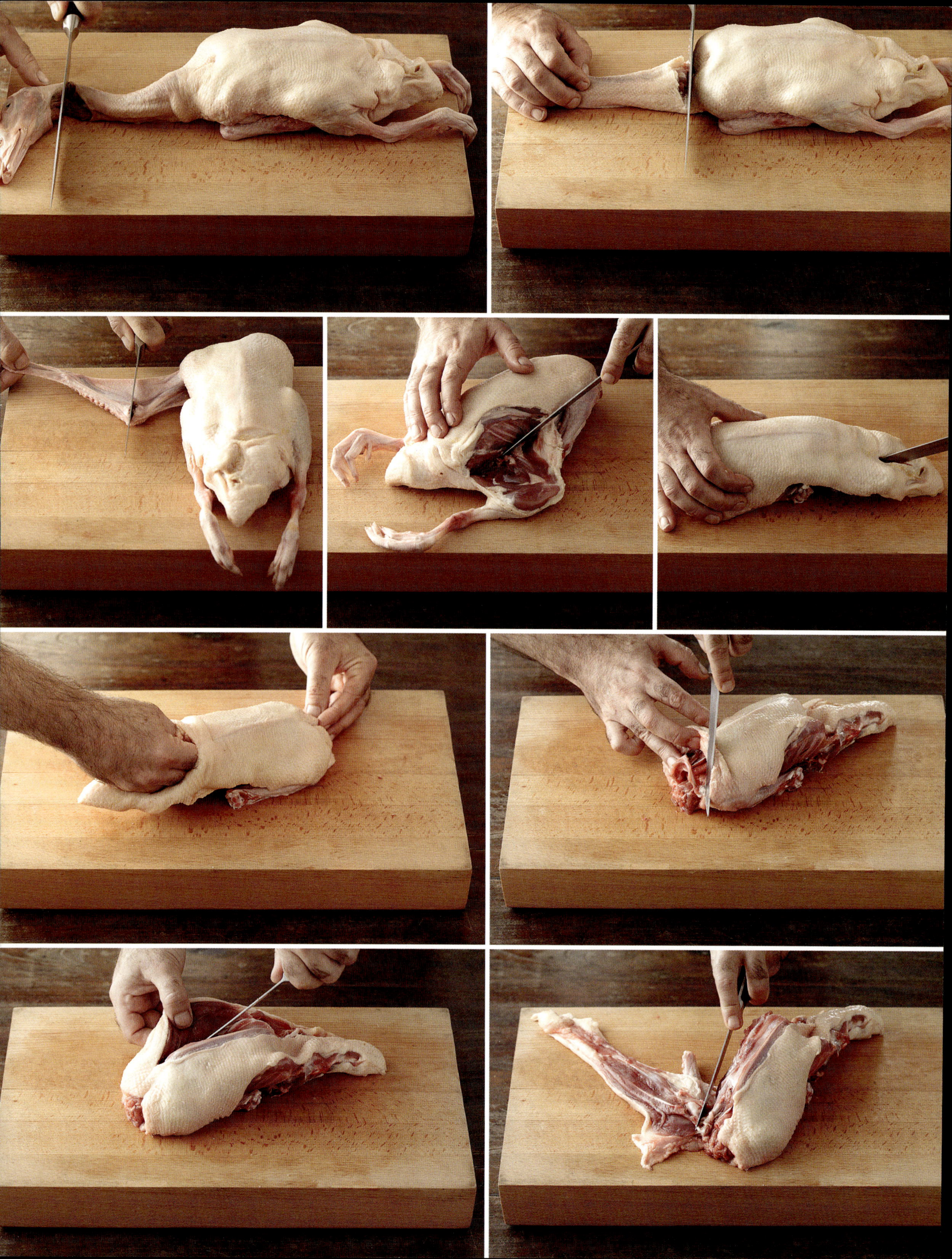

Cured Duck Breast

Makes 4

Air-drying meat and fish is one of the most ancient preserving methods. Serve as part of a hors d'oeuvre or charcuterie selection, or put thin slices in a salad. As well as adding flavour to the duck breasts, the salt starts the curing process by drawing out moisture, and helps prevent bacterial growth.

4 **duck breasts**

Salt Rub

100 g	**Maldon sea salt**
½	**stick cinnamon**
2	**cloves garlic, peeled**
4	**sprigs fresh thyme**
1	**sprig fresh rosemary**
½	**dried bay leaf**
1	**star anise**
2	**juniper berries, crushed**
2	**white peppercorns, crushed**
4	**coriander seeds, crushed**
1	**piece orange peel, pith removed**

Place all of the ingredients for the rub in a mortar and pound until crushed and aromatic. The salt will keep in an airtight container in the fridge for 2 weeks.

Trim the duck breasts of any excess skin and fat. Rub in the salt thoroughly. Place on a tray, cover with clingfilm and refrigerate overnight to allow them to marinate. The next day, wipe off all the salt from the duck breasts. Wrap each breast in a piece of muslin cloth and hang in a cool, dry place with good air circulation. Leave to cure for at least 7 days before using, until the breasts are firm and the flavour concentrated. Once cured, the duck will keep for 1 month in the fridge.

BASIC TECHNIQUE 12

Preparing and Cooking Confit

The word 'confit' means to preserve or conserve. The process of making confit involves cooking meat very slowly in fat, until it literally falls off the bone. The most common fats used for confit are from duck, goose or chicken, which are available commercially, but I recommend making your own as it is a very simple process.

RENDERING FAT

To make 1 litre of fat you will need to start with 2 kg of raw fat available from a good butcher. Place the fat in a heavy-based saucepan with 100 ml cold water to prevent the fat from sticking to the saucepan – the water will evaporate during cooking. Add 2 sprigs fresh rosemary, 2 sprigs fresh thyme, 2 crushed cloves garlic and 12 each crushed white peppercorns and coriander seeds. Place the fat over a very low heat and render for 6–8 hours. When the fat is crystal clear, pass it through a fine chinois into a stainless steel container. The fat can be used straightaway or stored, covered, in the fridge where it will solidify and can be kept for several months. When ready to use the fat, simply melt it down over a very low heat until it is crystal clear again.

I recommend to confit all poultry legs such as quail, squab, guinea fowl, pheasant, turkey or duck because they can be tough when roasted on the bone and contain a lot of sinew, which breaks down after the slow cooking process of confit. I also like to confit other meats with a low fat content, such as loin of pork or rabbit.

SALTING DUCK

Before the meat is made into confit it must be salted and left in the fridge for a few hours or overnight, depending on the size of the meat; quail, squab legs and duck gizzards will only need 2 hours whilst larger cuts like duck or chicken will take 12 hours. The salt will extract any moisture in the meat, which allows the meat to be stored for several months in its fat.

To salt 2 kg of meat you will need:

175 g	**coarse salt**
1	**star anise**
12	**coriander seeds**
12	**white peppercorns**
1	**stick cinnamon**
1	**dried bay leaf**
2	**sprigs fresh thyme**
6	**cloves garlic, peeled and crushed**
	zest of ½ orange

Using a pestle and mortar, crush the salt, star anise, coriander seeds, white peppercorns and cinnamon. Transfer to a bowl and add the bay leaf, thyme, garlic and orange zest. Rub the salt mix into the meat and place onto a perforated tray with another tray beneath to collect any moisture released from the meat. Refrigerate as explained above.

COOKING THE CONFIT

Rub the salt off the legs using a clean cloth. Preheat the oven to 120 °C. Place the meat in a heavy-based saucepan and cover with rendered fat. Heat the fat until it just simmers. Transfer to the oven and cook until the meat is soft and comes away from the bone. Duck legs will take 3–3½ hours, depending on their size, and smaller pieces of meat like duck gizzards will take 45–60 minutes. It is important that the temperature of the fat stays the same during cooking. If it gets too hot, this will result in fried, stringy and dry meat. Remove the confit from the oven and allow the meat to sit in the fat for 1 hour to cool slightly.

PRESSING THE DUCK CONFIT

Using a perforated spoon, carefully lift out the confit from the cooled fat, piece by piece, and place onto a clean tray. Allow the duck confit to cool sufficiently to be handled. Carefully remove the bones by gently twisting them. They will come away from the meat easily.

Place the legs onto a tray with a space between each one. Once the tray is full, cover the duck legs with a sheet of greaseproof paper and then place another tray on top of the paper. Place a 5 kg weight evenly across the tray to press the legs. Place the tray in the fridge and allow the legs to cool before removing the weight. When the duck legs are cold, trim up the sides to form even squares of duck confit.

STORING THE CONFIT

Using a perforated spoon, carefully lift out the confit from the fat, piece by piece, and place into a clean stainless steel or earthenware dish, gently layering the pieces on top of one another. Pass the fat through a fine sieve over the meat, covering it completely to form an airtight seal. Place the confit in the fridge where the fat will solidify. It can be kept for up to 6 months.

Duck Rillettes

Serves 8

275 g	**picked duck confit, skin and bones removed (*Basic Technique 12, page 168*)**
25 ml	**rendered duck fat (*Basic Technique 12, page 168*)**
15 ml	**sliced chives**
15 ml	**julienne of flat-leaf parsley**
25 g	**gherkins, chopped**
25 g	**cocktail onions, chopped**
	grated fresh horseradish to taste
40 ml	**Red Wine Jus (*Basic Recipe 12, page 42*)**
15 ml	**cognac**
	salt
	freshly ground pepper

Using your fingertips, shred the duck confit into a large bowl. Melt the duck fat and mix through the duck. Add the sliced chives, flat-leaf parsley, gherkins, cocktail onions and the horseradish to taste. Fold through the duck meat, taking care not to overwork the mixture. Add the red wine jus and cognac and season to taste with salt and freshly ground pepper.

Line a tray with a sheet of silicone and place 8 ring moulds (7 cm diameter, 1.5 cm deep) onto the sheet. Divide the rillette mix between the moulds so that the moulds are three-quarters full. Using a palette knife, spread and level out the rillettes so that the surfaces are flat and even. Transfer to the fridge for 15 minutes to allow the fat to set. Once the rillettes are firm, spoon over a thin layer of melted, rendered duck fat to cover the surface of each rillette.

Check the level of the fat after 15 minutes. If the rillettes are not packed tightly into the moulds, this may allow for some of the fat to seep through and they may need to be topped up with more fat. Refrigerate the rillettes until the fat is set before unmoulding.

Serve with toasted sourdough bread.

Duck Sausage with Warm Potato Salad and Aïoli

Makes 4 sausages

Duck Neck Sausage Filling

25 ml	**rendered duck fat (*Basic Technique 12, page 168*) or butter**
50 g	**brunoise of pancetta**
2	**shallots, peeled and finely chopped**
1	**clove garlic, peeled and finely chopped**
30 ml	**Madeira wine**
60 ml	**port**
50 ml	**Veal Jus (*Basic Recipe 11, page 41*)**
500 g	**minced duck meat with skin and sinew removed**
100 g	**picked duck confit (*Basic Technique 12, page 168*)**
1	**free-range egg**
12	**pistachio nuts, peeled**
10 g	**mixed herbs such as chopped flat-leaf parsley, sliced chives and picked thyme**
10 ml	**Maldon sea salt**
5 ml	**freshly ground white pepper**
4	**duck neck skins, cleaned with windpipes removed**
1.5 L	**water**
	vegetable oil

Warm Potato Salad

160 g	**baby potatoes**
25 ml	**extra virgin olive oil**
24	**lardons of pancetta**
1	**large shallot, peeled and thinly sliced**
	salt
	freshly ground pepper
100 ml	**Aïoli (*page 66*)**
	Deep-Fried Shallots (*Basic Technique 16, page 182*)
15 ml	**sliced chives**

First prepare the potatoes for the salad. Scrub the skins of the potatoes under cold water and cook in salted water over medium heat until tender. Allow to cool before peeling and cutting into 5 mm slices. Refrigerate until ready to use.

Next make the sausage. Melt the duck fat in a heavy-based pan over gentle heat and sauté the pancetta until golden brown. Add the shallots and garlic and continue to cook for another minute.

Mix the Madeira and port together in a saucepan and reduce by two-thirds. Add the veal jus and bring to the boil. Remove from the heat and set aside to cool.

Mix the minced duck meat, confit, pancetta, shallots, garlic, egg, pistachios and herbs to bind, and then mix in the reduced alcohol and veal jus. Season with salt and ground white pepper.

Secure each duck neck skin at one end with kitchen twine. Spoon the sausage filling into the skins until four-fifths full, leaving a little space for the mixture to expand during cooking. Pack the filling firmly to remove any air and tie the open ends with twine.

Bring the water to the boil in a large heavy-based saucepan. Reduce the heat to a simmer and add the sausages. Cook for 30 minutes, turning the sausages occasionally to ensure even cooking. It is important that the water does not boil as the sausages will split. Remove the sausages with a slotted spoon and refrigerate until cold before proceeding to the next stage.

Preheat the oven to 180 °C. Heat a little vegetable oil in a heavy-based pan over medium heat. Add the duck sausages and seal for 3–4 minutes until the skin is evenly browned all over. Transfer to the oven and continue to cook for a further 10 minutes until golden. Remove the sausages from the pan and place them onto a wire rack. Spoon the pan juices over them. Allow the sausages to rest for at least 10 minutes before carving each one into 6 even slices.

Continue making the potato salad. Heat the olive oil in a heavy-based pan, add the lardons of pancetta and cook until golden brown. Add the shallot and sliced potatoes and cook until lightly coloured. Lightly season with salt and freshly ground pepper. Remove from the pan and transfer to a sieve to allow the excess oil to drain off. Place the warm potato salad into a bowl and mix through 20 ml of the aïoli.

Place an 11 cm pastry ring in the centre of each of 4 plates and spoon the potato salad into it, pressing down with the back of the spoon so that it holds together. Arrange 6 overlapping slices of the duck neck sausage to form a neat circle on top of the potato salad. Gently remove the pastry ring. Drizzle the remaining aïoli over and around the duck. Garnish with deep-fried shallots and sliced chives.

VEGETABLES

BASIC TECHNIQUE 13

Tomato Concassée

Score the tomatoes and blanch in boiling water for 10 seconds, or until the skin begins to come away from the tomatoes. Remove from the water and plunge into iced water to halt the cooking process. Peel the skin and cut each tomato into quarters. Remove the seeds. Trim all four sides of the tomato quarters to give an even, rectangular piece of tomato. Slice the tomato into even-width strips lengthways and then cut across at the same width to make tomato concassée. If using the tomato concassée in a cold dish, season it lightly with salt, freshly ground pepper and a drizzle of olive oil. If adding the tomato concassée to a hot sauce, soup or consommé, do so at the last moment to prevent the tomato from becoming overcooked and mushy and from discolouring the liquid.

BASIC TECHNIQUE 14

Semi-Dried Tomatoes

Makes 24 pieces

70 ml	**cabernet sauvignon vinegar**
70 ml	**extra virgin olive oil**
5 ml	**sugar**
1	**branch fresh basil, roughly chopped**
1	**small sprig fresh rosemary**
1	**sprig fresh thyme**
½	**dried bay leaf**
	salt
	freshly ground pepper
12	**ripe plum tomatoes**

Mix together the vinegar, oil, sugar and herbs in a bowl and lightly season with salt and freshly ground pepper. Allow to infuse at room temperature for 1 hour.

Score the tomatoes and blanch in boiling water for 10–15 seconds, or until the skins start to come away (*Basic Technique 13, see above*). Refresh in iced water. Peel the tomatoes and cut in half lengthways. Remove the seeds using a teaspoon. Place the tomatoes in the marinade for 30 minutes.

Preheat the oven to the lowest possible setting. Remove the tomatoes from the marinade and place onto a wire rack to drain. Place the rack onto a baking tray and then into the oven for 2½–3 hours. The tomatoes will have shrunk in size and become more intense in flavour but should still be moist. It is important that the tomatoes are dried at a low temperature. If too hot, the tomatoes will become too dry, discolour and lose their flavour. If not using the tomatoes immediately, refrigerate covered in extra virgin olive oil with a crushed garlic clove and a few sprigs of basil and thyme until ready to use. The tomatoes will keep for 3–4 days in the fridge.

Picture on next page

Blanching Sweet Peppers (Capsicum)

Heat 1 litre vegetable oil to 120 °C in a heavy-based pan over a low heat. Place the whole peppers into the oil and, using a long-handled spoon, turn them until the skins start to blister. Do not allow the peppers to colour. When the skins are blistered, remove the peppers from the oil, place into a bowl and cover with clingfilm. The peppers will steam in their own heat and the skins will loosen after 15 minutes. Place the peppers on a chopping board and, using a sharp knife, cut them through the centre and open up like a book, keeping them in one piece. Remove the stalks and seeds. Turn the peppers over and scrape off the skins with the tip of a knife. The peppers can be kept for 5–6 days in a little olive oil with fresh herbs and crushed garlic until ready to use.

Deep-Fried Shallots

500 ml	vegetable oil for deep-frying
4	shallots, peeled and sliced
	salt
	freshly ground pepper

Heat the oil to 170 °C in a heavy-based saucepan. Add the shallots. Stir frequently and cook until crisp and golden. Remove from the heat and lift the shallots out of the oil using a slotted spoon. Drain on kitchen paper to absorb any excess oil. Season to taste with salt and freshly ground pepper. When the oil has cooled, pass it through a fine sieve into a clean container until ready to use again.

Deep-Fried Chillies

4	medium-sized red chillies
500 ml	vegetable oil for deep-frying
	salt
	freshly ground pepper

Halve the chillies, remove the stalks and seeds and slice thinly. Heat the oil to 180 °C in a heavy-based saucepan and then add the sliced chillies. Stir frequently and cook until crisp. Remove from the heat and lift the chillies out of the oil using a slotted spoon. Drain on kitchen paper to absorb any excess oil. Season to taste with salt and freshly ground pepper. When the oil has cooled, pass it through a fine sieve into a clean container until ready to use again.

Deep-Fried Parsnip Chips

2	medium parsnips
500 ml	vegetable oil for deep-frying
	salt
	freshly ground pepper

Peel the parsnips, top and tail them and slice thinly on a mandoline. Heat the oil to 180 °C in a heavy-based saucepan and then add the parsnips. Stir frequently and cook until they are crisp and golden brown. Remove from the heat and lift the parsnip chips out of the oil using a slotted spoon. Drain on kitchen paper to absorb any excess oil. Season to taste with salt and freshly ground pepper. When the oil has cooled, pass it through a fine sieve into a clean container until ready to use again.

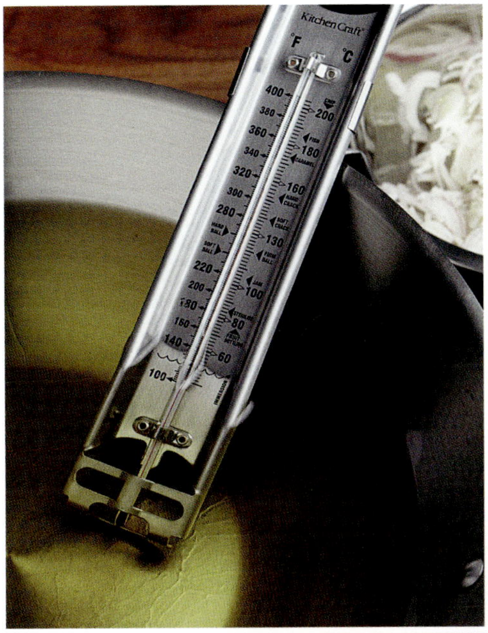
KitchenCraft

BASIC TECHNIQUE 17

Preparing and Cooking Asparagus

Only buy firm, crisp asparagus. Cut 2–3 cm off the woody base of the asparagus spears, depending on their size. Using a swivel peeler, peel the outer skin from just under the tip down to the base. Discard the skin. Cook the asparagus in boiling salted water until tender – this will take 1–1½ minutes, depending on the thickness of the asparagus. Check it with the tip of a knife. If not serving the asparagus immediately, refresh in iced water to stop the cooking process. Drain and place on a clean tea towel and store covered in the fridge until ready to use.

BASIC TECHNIQUE 18

Preparing and Cooking Beetroot

Beetroot come in bunches with edible leaves at the top when young, and loose and trimmed when mature. When buying raw beetroot make sure that they have at least 5 cm of stalk at the top – if they are too closely trimmed they will bleed, meaning they will give up most of their colour to the cooking liquid. For the same reason, beetroot are never peeled before they are cooked. The leaves of young beetroot can be served raw in a salad or can be blanched and served as a vegetable; it tastes similar to English spinach. Golden and white beetroot are also available and taste the same as the red variety.

8	**medium beetroot, stalks removed**
3 L	**water**
200 ml	**verjuice**
100 ml	**chardonnay vinegar**
	pinch saffron threads
80 g	**sugar**
5 ml	**salt**
	freshly ground pepper

Scrub the beetroot under cold running water. Place them in a medium pan and add the remaining ingredients. Poach gently, uncovered, for 2 hours, or until the beetroot are tender. Remove from the heat and allow to cool slightly in the poaching liquor. When cool enough to handle, peel the beetroot.

Pour the poaching liquor through a fine sieve lined with muslin cloth. Bring 250 ml of the strained liquor to the boil, lower the heat and reduce by two-thirds to a syrupy consistency. Remove from the heat and allow to cool. Pass the liquid through a fine sieve and use to dress beetroot salad (*page 86*).

BASIC TECHNIQUE 19

Mushroom Duxelle

Makes 250 g

It is important that the pan in which the mushrooms are sautéed maintains its heat, otherwise the mushrooms will release their juice and end up boiling in it, losing colour and a lot of flavour.

25 g	dried cep mushrooms
200 g	button mushrooms
50 ml	olive oil
1	clove garlic, crushed
4	sprigs fresh thyme
1	small shallot, peeled and finely chopped
	salt
	freshly ground pepper
15 ml	sliced chives

Soften and reconstitute the dried cep mushrooms in warm water for 4 hours. Remove from the water and drain. Trim the stalks of the button mushrooms, wipe them with a damp cloth and cut into quarters. Heat the olive oil in a large cast-iron pan until smoking. Add the button mushrooms, soaked cep mushrooms, garlic, thyme and shallots and sauté until golden brown. Season with salt and freshly ground pepper. (Sauté the mushrooms in 2 batches if the pan is not large enough.) Drain the mushrooms and remove the garlic and thyme. When cold, chop the mushrooms very finely, almost to a purée.

To serve, reheat the mushroom duxelle in a heavy-based saucepan over low heat. Add the sliced chives and stir through. Adjust the seasoning if necessary.

BASIC RECIPE 38

Roasted Vegetables

Serves 4

2	large parsnips, peeled, topped and tailed
2	large carrots, peeled, topped and tailed
30 ml	olive oil
12	cloves garlic, skin on
12	shallots, peeled
	salt
	freshly ground pepper
30 g	unsalted butter
3	large sprigs fresh thyme

Preheat the oven to 180 °C. Cut the parsnips and carrots into 5 cm lengths and then slice into 1 cm thick batons. Heat the olive oil in a cast-iron pan over medium heat and add the parsnips, carrots, garlic and shallots. Season with salt and freshly ground pepper and cook until they are evenly caramelised. Transfer the pan to the oven and continue to cook for a further 4–5 minutes, or until the parsnips are tender. Turn the vegetables occasionally so that they remain evenly coloured. Add the butter and thyme for the last 2 minutes of cooking. Remove the vegetables from the oven, drain and remove the thyme and garlic. Adjust the seasoning if necessary.

BASIC RECIPE 39

Garlic Purée

Makes 150 g

24	cloves garlic, peeled
1	sprig fresh thyme
	Clarified Butter to cover (*Basic Recipe 10, page 39*)
	salt
	freshly ground pepper

Place the garlic and thyme in a heavy-based saucepan and cover with clarified butter. Gently cook the garlic until tender over a very low heat for 30–35 minutes. Drain the garlic and pass it through a fine drum sieve. Season to taste with salt and freshly ground pepper.

Alternatively, the garlic can be kept in its skin and lightly coated in olive oil. Season with salt and freshly ground pepper and wrap in aluminium foil with a large sprig of thyme. Cook in an oven at 140 °C for 35–40 minutes until the garlic is tender. Allow the garlic to cool. Remove it from the skin and pass through a drum sieve. Season the purée with salt and freshly ground pepper to taste.

If not using the garlic purée immediately, place in a bowl and cover with a thin film of extra virgin olive oil to prevent it from discolouring. Pass the clarified butter through a fine sieve until ready to use again.

Garlic Confit

Makes 24 pieces

24	cloves garlic, peeled
1	sprig fresh thyme
	salt
	freshly ground pepper
250 g	Clarified Butter (*Basic Recipe 10, page 39*) or rendered duck fat (*Basic Technique 12, page 168*)

Place the garlic and thyme in a heavy-based saucepan and season with salt and freshly ground pepper. Cover with either clarified butter or duck fat. Gently cook the garlic over a very low heat for 30–35 minutes until tender. Remove from the heat and allow to cool in the fat. Refrigerate until ready to use. The garlic cloves can be stored for up to a week in the fridge.

ROAST GARLIC

To roast, drain the garlic from the fat. Heat a little of the fat in a heavy-based pan. Add the garlic and cook until golden brown. Lightly season with salt and freshly ground pepper. Drain the garlic before serving.

BASIC RECIPE 40

Creamed Spinach

Makes 250 g

1.5 kg	English spinach or baby spinach
140 ml	fresh cream
1	clove garlic, crushed
	salt
	freshly ground pepper
25 g	Shallot Confit (*page 193*)

Pick the spinach, discarding the stalks. Wash the spinach in several changes of cold water to remove any grit or sand. Blanch the spinach in boiling salted water for 1 minute. Plunge into iced water to stop the cooking process. Drain the spinach, squeeze out the water and chop finely. Place the cream in a saucepan with the crushed garlic and season with a little salt and freshly ground pepper. Reduce by two-thirds over medium heat, then remove from the heat and pass it through a fine sieve, discarding the garlic. To serve, reheat the cream in a saucepan, add the spinach and shallot confit and gently warm through. Season to taste with salt and freshly ground pepper.

P
S

BASIC RECIPE 41

Braised Shallots

Serves 4

50 g	unsalted butter
24	shallots, peeled
10 ml	sherry vinegar
	salt
	freshly ground pepper
150 ml	Veal Stock (*Basic Recipe 4, page 14*)
2	sprigs fresh thyme

Melt the butter in a heavy-based pan over medium heat until the butter is foaming. Add the shallots and sauté until they are evenly golden brown. Add the sherry vinegar and cook until it evaporates, and then season with salt and freshly ground pepper. Add the veal stock and thyme and bring to the boil. Reduce the heat, cover the pan with greaseproof paper and simmer gently for 15–20 minutes until the shallots are tender. Test with the tip of a knife, take the pan off the heat and keep the shallots warm in the stock until ready to serve.

Shallot Confit

Makes 500 g

500 g	shallots, finely chopped
1	sprig fresh thyme
	salt
	freshly ground pepper
250 ml	Clarified Butter (*Basic Recipe 10, page 39*)

Place the shallots and thyme in a heavy-based saucepan. Season with salt and freshly ground pepper and cover with clarified butter. Gently cook the shallots over a very low heat for 25–30 minutes until tender. Remove from the heat and allow to cool in the clarified butter. Refrigerate until ready to use. The shallots can be stored for up to a week before using.

BASIC RECIPE 42

Braised Red Cabbage

Makes 500 g

1	head red cabbage (500 g)
½	stick cinnamon
6	juniper berries
325 ml	cabernet sauvignon
50 ml	port
125 ml	cabernet sauvignon vinegar
	juice of 1 orange
25 ml	brown sugar
	salt
	freshly ground pepper
100 g	unsalted butter

Remove any wilted or damaged leaves from the cabbage. Cut into quarters and remove the core. Using a sharp knife, slice the cabbage as thinly as possible and place into a deep tray. Tie up the cinnamon and juniper berries in a piece of muslin cloth and add to the cabbage. Add the remaining ingredients, except the butter, and mix well. Cover with clingfilm and marinate in the fridge for 12 hours.

Preheat the oven to 140 °C. Drain the cabbage and reserve the liquid. Melt the butter in a heavy-based saucepan, add the cabbage and cook without colour until it wilts down. Add the reserved liquid and bring to the boil. Cover the saucepan with a lid and transfer the cabbage to the oven. Cook for 2½–3 hours until the cabbage is tender and the juices have reduced to a syrup. Stir every 30 minutes. Remove the muslin bag from the cabbage and discard. Check the seasoning and adjust if necessary. Add a little more cabernet sauvignon vinegar if necessary. The cabbage can be kept covered in the fridge for 4–5 days before using.

BASIC RECIPE 43

Lyonnaise Onions

Makes 300 g

1.5 kg	brown onions
75 g	unsalted butter
	salt
	freshly ground pepper

Peel the onions, cut in half and slice as thinly as possible. Melt the butter in a heavy-based saucepan over medium heat. When it foams, reduce the heat and add the onions. Cook for 2½–3 hours over a very low heat until all the water released from the onions has evaporated. The onions will caramelise and take on a deep, golden brown colour. Season to taste with salt and freshly ground pepper. If not using immediately, spread the onions on a tray and refrigerate to cool. Reheat over a very low heat when ready to use.

BASIC RECIPE 44

Petit Pois à la Française

Serves 4

150 g	shelled peas
20 ml	rendered duck fat (*Basic Technique 12, page 168*) or olive oil
40 g	pancetta, finely diced
4	shallots, peeled and finely diced
100 ml	Chicken Stock (*Basic Recipe 1, page 12*)
20 g	unsalted butter, diced
1	small cos lettuce, shredded
	salt
	freshly ground pepper

Blanch the peas in plenty of boiling salted water until they rise to the surface. Transfer them to a bowl of iced water to halt the cooking process.

Heat the duck fat or olive oil in a heavy-based saucepan over medium heat. Add the pancetta and shallots and sauté until they are lightly coloured. Strain the peas and add to the saucepan. Add the chicken stock and bring to the boil. Add the butter and stir gently until the butter is fully incorporated. Add the cos lettuce and toss through the peas until it begins to wilt. Season to taste with salt and freshly ground pepper.

Tomato and Olive Tarts

Serves 4

Tomato Tarts

200 g	Rough Puff Pastry (*Basic Recipe 61, page 240*)
8	Roma tomatoes, blanched and peeled
120 g	Tapenade (*Basic Recipe 37, page 74*)
	egg wash of free-range egg and 10 ml milk
	salt
	freshly ground pepper
8	cherry tomatoes
8	yellow teardrop tomatoes
24	slices black olive
12	baby basil leaves
12	chive tips
12	sprigs fresh chervil
12	mache leaves
20 ml	extra virgin olive oil

Marinade

50 ml	cabernet sauvignon vinegar
50 ml	extra virgin olive oil
	pinch sugar
1	branch fresh basil, roughly chopped
1	small sprig fresh rosemary
1	sprig fresh thyme
½	dried bay leaf
	salt
	freshly ground pepper

Make the marinade for the Roma tomatoes: Mix the cabernet sauvignon vinegar, olive oil, sugar, chopped basil, rosemary, thyme and bay leaf together in a bowl and lightly season with salt and freshly ground pepper. Allow to infuse at room temperature for 1 hour.

Lightly dust a work surface with flour and roll out the pastry to a thickness of 5 mm. Using a 10 cm pastry cutter, cut out 4 circles of pastry. Place the pastry circles on a cold baking tray and prick with a fork. Rest the pastry in the fridge for 30 minutes.

Cut the Roma tomatoes into 5 mm slices and place them in a bowl. Pour the tomato marinade over the sliced tomatoes so that they are evenly coated. Allow to marinate for 30 minutes at room temperature.

Preheat the oven to 200 °C. Remove the puff pastry circles from the fridge. Place an 8 cm pastry cutter in the centre of each pastry circle and, using a small palette knife, spread 10 ml tapenade inside the pastry cutter. Brush the 2 cm rim with the egg wash. Arrange 8 slices of marinated tomato on top of the tapenade in a circle, overlapping each other. Lightly season the tomato with salt and freshly ground pepper. Lightly spray another baking tray with water and transfer the tomato tarts onto this tray. Place the tarts in the oven and cook for 8 minutes until the pastry is crisp and golden.

While the tarts are cooking, cut the cherry and teardrop tomatoes in half and lightly season with salt and freshly ground pepper. Warm them under a salamander or in the oven for 2 minutes. Using 2 teaspoons, make 4 quenelles with the remainder of the tapenade.

Check that the tart bases are cooked before removing from the oven. Place a tart in the centre of a warmed plate. Place the cherry and teardrop tomatoes and olive slices around the sides of the tart. Place a quenelle of tapenade in the centre of the tart and garnish with the basil, chives, chervil and mache leaves. Drizzle a little of the olive oil around the plate.

PULSES, PASTA, RICE AND GRAINS

BASIC RECIPE 45

Lentilles du Puys

Serves 4

Stage 1

150 g Puy lentils
500 ml Chicken Stock (*Basic Recipe 1, page 12*)
2 small carrots, peeled and halved lengthways
1 onion, peeled and cut into 8 wedges
1 small leek, cut into 4 lengthways
1 stick celery, halved lengthways
1 sprig fresh thyme

Place the lentils in a sieve and rinse under cold running water. Drain the lentils, place in a heavy-based saucepan and cover with cold water. Bring to the boil, remove from the heat, drain and refresh under cold running water.

Pour 250 ml chicken stock and 250 ml water into a heavy-based saucepan. Add the refreshed lentils, vegetables and thyme. Stir, then cover with a piece of greaseproof paper and bring to the boil. Reduce the heat and simmer gently for 5–8 minutes until the lentils are half-cooked. Drain the lentils in a sieve and discard the vegetables and thyme.

Stage 2

10 ml olive oil
50 g diced pancetta
3 shallots, peeled and very finely chopped
½ stick celery, strings removed and finely diced
½ carrot, peeled and finely diced
100 g cold unsalted butter, diced
45 ml chopped mixed herbs, including parsley, chervil and chives
salt
freshly ground pepper

Heat the olive oil in a deep heavy-based saucepan over medium heat. Add the diced pancetta and finely chopped vegetables and sweat without colour for 3 minutes.

Add the lentils to the saucepan and pour in the remaining chicken stock. Reduce the heat and simmer gently, uncovered, for 10 minutes until the liquid has reduced by half.

Stir in the butter, a cube or two at a time, until it is fully incorporated, then stir in the fresh herbs and season to taste with salt and pepper.

BASIC RECIPE 46

Fresh Pasta

Makes 880 g

500 g	Italian '00' pasta flour, sifted twice
	salt
300 ml	egg mix (consists of 3 whole free-range eggs and the remainder made up with egg yolks)
20 ml	olive oil
60 ml	water

Place the flour into the bowl of a food processor (or mix by hand) with a good pinch of salt. Whisk the eggs and egg yolks until liquefied. With the motor running, add the egg, olive oil and water in a steady stream and continue to run the motor until the dough comes away from the sides of the bowl. Turn out the dough onto a lightly floured work surface and knead for 5 minutes until smooth. Wrap the pasta in clingfilm and refrigerate for 1 hour.

Cut the pasta dough into 2 pieces. Roll out both pieces with a rolling pin on a lightly floured work surface until they are 5 mm thick. Set a pasta machine on the thickest setting and feed through the first piece of pasta twice. Adjust the setting one notch and feed through the pasta twice again. Continue to roll the pasta until it is on the thinnest setting. Treat the second piece in the same way. When all the pasta is rolled, cut it to desired lengths or shapes. Place the pasta on a plate and cover with clingfilm to prevent it from drying out.

Saffron Pasta Dough

Makes 900 g

250 ml	water
5 ml	saffron threads
5 ml	saffron powder
500 g	Italian '00' pasta flour, sifted twice
	salt
300 g	free-range egg yolks
20 ml	olive oil

Place the water, saffron threads and powder into a heavy-based saucepan over low heat and reduce to 50 ml. Remove from the heat and allow to cool, then pass the saffron liquid through a fine chinois into a clean bowl, pressing down on the saffron with the back of a spoon to extract as much colour and flavour as possible.

Place the flour into the bowl of a food processor (or mix by hand) with a good pinch of salt. Whisk the egg yolks until liquefied. With the motor running, add the saffron liquid, egg yolks and the olive oil in a steady stream and continue to run the motor until the dough comes away from the sides of the bowl. Turn out the dough onto a work surface and knead for 5 minutes until smooth. Wrap the pasta in clingfilm and refrigerate for 1 hour before rolling out using a pasta machine (*see above*).

Squid Ink Pasta Dough

Makes 420 g

250 g	**Italian '00' pasta flour, sifted twice**
	salt
90 g	**egg mix (consists of 1 whole free-range egg and the remainder made up with egg yolks)**
60 g	**squid ink**
10 ml	**olive oil**

Place the flour into the bowl of a food processor (or mix by hand) with a good pinch of salt. Whisk the egg, egg yolks and squid ink until liquefied. With the motor running, pour in the egg and ink mix and olive oil in a steady stream and continue to run the motor until the dough comes away from the sides of the bowl. Turn out the dough onto a work surface and knead for 5 minutes until smooth. Wrap the pasta in clingfilm and refrigerate for 1 hour before rolling out using a pasta machine (*page 200*).

BASIC RECIPE 47

Potato Gnocchi, Asparagus and Pancetta

Serves 4

Potato Gnocchi

600 g	large Sebago potatoes, washed (or any potato suitable for baking)
150 g	Italian '00' pasta flour, sifted
60 g	Parmesan cheese, freshly grated
3	free-range egg yolks
60 ml	olive oil
	salt
	freshly ground pepper

For Serving

15 ml	olive oil
100 g	lardons of pancetta
20 g	chilled unsalted butter, diced
12	asparagus spears, peeled, blanched and refreshed (*Basic Technique 17, page 184*)

Preheat the oven to 180 °C. Place the potatoes on a baking tray and bake in the oven for 70–90 minutes until tender, depending on their size. Remove the potatoes from the oven and cut in half. Using a spoon, scoop out the flesh and pass it through a drum sieve. Weigh out 550 g potato purée and place into a bowl. Add the flour, Parmesan cheese, egg yolks and olive oil and work into a dough. Season to taste with salt and pepper. Turn out the dough onto a lightly floured work surface and knead for 3 minutes. If it feels wet, add a little more flour. The dough should be soft but not sticky. Spoon the dough into a piping bag fitted with a 3 cm plain tube and pipe out lines onto a lightly floured surface. Cut the gnocchi into 3 cm lengths.

Bring a large saucepan of salted water to the boil and cook the gnocchi in several batches. Simply drop the gnocchi into the water and, when they float to the surface after 3–4 minutes, lift them from the water and plunge into iced water to refresh. When cold, drain them from the water and dry on a clean tea towel. If not using the gnocchi immediately, mix through 20 ml olive oil to prevent them from sticking together. Keep the gnocchi covered in the fridge until required.

To serve, heat a heavy-based frying pan over medium heat and add the olive oil. When hot, add the gnocchi and sauté for 3–4 minutes until golden brown. Add the lardons and continue to cook until nicely browned. Add the butter and asparagus and continue to cook for a further 2 minutes. Drain the gnocchi, check the seasoning and adjust if necessary. Divide the gnocchi between 4 warmed bowls.

Soft Polenta

Serves 4

500 ml	**Chicken Stock (*Basic Recipe 1, page 12*)**
150 ml	**milk**
150 ml	**fresh cream**
4	**cloves garlic, peeled**
4	**dried cep mushrooms**
1	**sprig fresh thyme**
1	**dried bay leaf**
1	**sprig fresh rosemary**
1	**shallot, peeled and sliced**
350 g	**polenta**
	salt
	freshly ground pepper
50 g	**Parmesan cheese, freshly grated**

In a heavy-based saucepan, bring the chicken stock, milk, cream, garlic, cep mushrooms, thyme, bay leaf, rosemary and sliced shallot to the boil. Reduce the heat and simmer for 10 minutes. Remove from the heat and allow to infuse for 1 hour.

Pass the infused stock through a fine sieve into a clean saucepan. Return to the heat and bring back to the boil. Reduce the heat so that the stock just simmers. Pour in the polenta in a steady stream, stirring vigorously to prevent any lumps from forming. Continue to stir while cooking over gentle heat for 10–12 minutes. The polenta will come away from the sides of the saucepan when it is cooked. Season to taste with salt and pepper and fold in the Parmesan cheese. Cook for 1 minute more and serve.

PAN-FRIED POLENTA

Line a tray with clingfilm, leaving a 10–15 cm overhang. Follow the recipe and method above to cook the polenta. Pour the cooked polenta into the tray and smooth over with a palette knife. Fold over the overhanging clingfilm to cover the top of the polenta. Refrigerate for at least 2 hours to set before turning out.

Run a sharp knife around the inside of the tray and invert onto a chopping board. Cut the polenta into even slices or cut out rounds with a pastry cutter.

Heat 20 ml olive oil in a non-stick pan, reduce to a gentle heat and place the polenta slices into the pan. Fry for 4–5 minutes until golden brown. Gently turn the polenta slices with a palette knife and fry for a further 4–5 minutes until golden brown and warmed through. Lightly season with salt and pepper. Serve with a garnish of your choice.

BASIC RECIPE 49

Mushroom Risotto

Serves 6 as a first course or 4 as a main course

Rice used for making risotto is grown in the Po Valley in the northern part of Italy. There are four different styles grown: ordinario, a short round grain; semifino, a medium-length grain; fino, a long grain rice; and superfino, the best type for risotto as it can be cooked slowly for a long period of time, has good absorption and maintains its shape during cooking. It is also very rich in starch, which is so important to the finished creamy texture of the risotto.

Types of risotto rice include Aborio, Vialoni nano, Vialoni nano gigante and Carnaroli. My preference is either the Aborio or Carnaroli.

After choosing the rice, the most important thing is the stock in which the risotto is going to be cooked. It must be full-flavoured and at simmering point. It is important that the stock is hot, as this breaks down the outside of the rice, releasing the starch which creates a creamy texture. Use a wide, heavy-based saucepan in which to make risotto to ensure even cooking of the rice.

If you have leftover risotto, pour it onto a clingfilm covered tray so it is 1 cm deep and smooth over with a palette knife. Allow it to solidify in the fridge. Use a 10 cm pastry cutter to cut out rounds of the cold risotto. Heat some Clarified Butter (*Basic Recipe 10, page 39*) in a non-stick pan and fry the risotto rounds until golden brown on both sides. Transfer to a preheated oven at 180 °C and reheat the risotto for 10 minutes. The risotto cakes will be crisp on the outside and soft and creamy in the centre.

1.2 L	**Mushroom or Chicken Stock (*Basic Recipe 8 or 1, page 20 or 12*)**
50 g	**unsalted butter**
1	**clove garlic, crushed**
100 g	**finely chopped onion**
250 g	**Aborio rice**
50 g	**chilled unsalted butter, diced**
50 g	**Parmesan cheese, freshly grated**
	salt
	freshly ground pepper
	truffle oil to taste (optional)
100 g	**fresh oyster mushrooms, sautéed**
100 g	**button mushrooms, sautéed**
50 g	**dried morel mushrooms, soaked in warm water for 15 minutes and drained, then sautéed**

Bring the stock to the boil in a heavy-based saucepan, and then reduce the heat so that the stock is just simmering.

In a large, heavy-based saucepan, melt the butter, add the garlic and onion and sweat without colour for 2 minutes. Add the Aborio rice and seal for a further 2 minutes without colour.

Add a ladle of stock and stir into the rice. Continue to cook, stirring the rice continuously to prevent it from sticking. Reduce the heat so that the rice simmers (too much heat will result in boiled rice) and continue to cook until the stock has been absorbed. Continue to add the stock a ladle at a time and cook the risotto until the rice softens (al dente), which will take 18–20 minutes.

To finish the risotto, add the chilled, diced butter and stir into the rice until fully incorporated. Add the Parmesan and fold through the risotto. Remove and discard the garlic clove. Season to taste with salt and pepper and truffle oil if using.

Add the sautéed mushrooms and fold through the risotto. Divide the risotto between warmed bowls and garnish with shaved Parmesan.

Roast Onion Risotto

Serves 6 as a first course or 4 as a main course

2	large onions
90 g	unsalted butter
45 ml	olive oil
1.2 L	Chicken Stock (*Basic Recipe 1, page 12*)
1	clove garlic, crushed
2	onions, peeled and finely chopped
250 g	Aborio rice
50 g	Parmesan cheese, grated
	salt
	freshly ground pepper
100 g	sliced spring onions
25 g	sliced chives

Preheat the oven to 140 °C. Take the 2 large onions and remove any loose skins. Cut the top off the onions. Heat 50 g of the butter and 20 ml of the olive oil in a heavy-based pan, place the onions into the pan, cut-side down, and gently cook until the onions caramelise and take on an even, golden brown colour. Transfer to the oven and roast for 1½–2 hours until the onions are soft and cooked through. Remove from the oven and allow to cool slightly before removing the roots and skins. Carefully remove the centres of the onions, leaving a shell in the original shape. Save the 6 best shells. Place the remaining onion into a blender with a little stock and blend to a purée. Pass through a sieve for a smooth onion purée. Set aside with the shells while you make the risotto.

Bring the chicken stock to the boil and then reduce the heat so that the stock just simmers. Heat the remaining 25 ml olive oil in a heavy-based saucepan and add the crushed garlic and chopped onions and sweat without colour for 2 minutes. Add the rice and seal without colour for a further 2 minutes. Add a ladle of chicken stock and stir into the rice. Continue to cook, stirring the rice to prevent it from sticking. Reduce the heat so that the rice just simmers and continue to cook until the stock has been absorbed. Add the stock, one ladle at a time, and cook the risotto until the rice is al dente, 15–18 minutes.

To finish the risotto, add 40 g diced butter and stir into the rice until fully incorporated, then add half of the Parmesan and fold through the risotto. Add the onion purée to taste. Remove and discard the garlic clove. Season to taste with salt and freshly ground pepper. Fold in the sliced spring onions and chives, remove from the heat and spoon into the onion shells. Fill to the top of the shells, sprinkle with the remaining Parmesan and serve.

Paella

Serves 4

250 g	black mussels
8	prawns in the shell
50 ml	white wine
750 ml	Chicken Stock (*Basic Recipe 1, page 12*)
1	large sprig fresh thyme
30 ml	olive oil
50 g	chorizo, diced into 5 mm cubes
12 ml	paprika
	pinch saffron threads
7.5 ml	dried oregano
	pinch dried chilli flakes
1	large onion, peeled and chopped
2	cloves garlic, peeled and chopped
1	bay leaf
1	sprig fresh thyme
1	large red pepper (capsicum), seeded and finely diced
1	large green pepper (capsicum), seeded and finely diced
2	ripe tomatoes, seeded and diced
400 g	rice
2	pieces orange zest
	salt
	freshly ground pepper
4	chicken thighs
15 ml	vegetable oil
60 g	peas, blanched and refreshed
1	small bunch flat-leaf parsley, finely chopped

Scrub and debeard the mussels. Rinse them under cold running water to remove any sand and grit. Discard any broken mussels (*Basic Technique 5, page 107*). Cover and refrigerate until ready to use. Cut each prawn in half, remove and discard the dark vein (*Basic Technique 1, page 89*). Cover and refrigerate until ready to use.

Bring the wine to the boil in a shallow saucepan, add the mussels, cover and bring back to the boil. Add 300 ml of the chicken stock and thyme and cook for 3–4 minutes until the mussels open, taking care not to overcook them. Remove from the heat and tip the mussels into a colander placed in a bowl to catch all of the stock. Cover the mussels with a damp cloth and set aside until ready to use. Pass the stock through a fine chinois and add to the remaining chicken stock.

Place a paella pan or shallow casserole dish over medium heat and add the olive oil. When hot, add the chorizo and fry, stirring until just coloured. Add the paprika, saffron, oregano, chilli flakes, onion, garlic, bay leaf, thyme, capsicums and diced tomatoes. Stir and cook for three minutes. Stir and cook for 3 minutes until the onion and garlic are softened. Add the rice and continue to cook and stir for a further 3 minutes.

Pour in the stock and stir in the orange zest, and lightly season with salt and freshly ground pepper. Bring to the boil, stirring occasionally. Reduce the heat to low and cook the paella uncovered for 15–18 minutes. From this point onwards, do not stir the paella, as a crust needs to form on the bottom of the pan. If the flame or element is too small to cover the base of the pan, move the pan around during cooking to allow the paella to cook evenly.

While the paella is cooking, cook the chicken thighs. Lightly season the chicken with salt, freshly ground pepper and paprika. Heat the vegetable oil in a heavy-based saucepan over medium heat. Place the chicken skin-side down in the pan and cook for 4–5 minutes until evenly browned and crisp. Turn the chicken over and cook for a further 2 minutes. Transfer the chicken to the paella, placing the pieces evenly around the pan.

When the majority of the stock has been absorbed and small holes appear between the rice (this will take 12 minutes), place the prawns on top, flesh-side down, and allow the escaping steam to gently cook them. Cook for a few minutes until the shells take on a light orange colour, then turn and cook the other side of the prawn. Add the peas and cook for a further 5 minutes. Spread the mussels evenly over the top of the paella. Remove the paella from the heat and cover with aluminium foil and allow the steam from the paella to finish cooking the rice and to reheat the mussels gently so they stay nice and moist. Sprinkle with parsley before serving.

Mango Couscous

Serves 4

200 g	couscous
250 ml	hot Chicken Stock (*Basic Recipe 1, page 12*)
30 ml	olive oil
1	clove garlic, minced
1	mango, peeled, pitted and cut into 1 cm dice
1	chilli, seeded and ribs removed, finely chopped
25 g	raisins, soaked in warm water
1	tomato, blanched, peeled and diced
30 ml	peeled pistachio nuts, chopped
30 ml	toasted cashew or almonds, roughly chopped
30 ml	chopped coriander
30 ml	chopped flat-leaf parsley
	juice of 1 lime
	salt
	freshly ground pepper

Place the couscous in a large bowl and stir in the hot chicken stock. As you pour in the hot stock, whisk constantly to separate the grains. Cover tightly with clingfilm and leave in a warm place for at least 30 minutes. Stir the couscous with a fork several times to separate the grains. At the end of soaking, the couscous will have increased in volume and the grains will be swollen and plump.

Heat 15 ml of the olive oil in a large pan over a high heat. Add the garlic, mango and chilli and sauté until the mango begins to colour slightly. Stir in the remaining olive oil, the couscous, raisins, tomato, nuts, coriander and parsley and toss to heat through. Add the lime juice to taste. Season with salt and freshly ground pepper to taste.

POTATOES

Hundreds of different varieties of potatoes are cultivated all over the world in a vast range of shapes, sizes, colours and textures ranging from 'mealy' and 'floury' to 'waxy'.

There are three categories of potatoes: waxy (low starch), starchy (high starch content) and all-purpose floury (between waxy and starchy).

The potato has endless versatility, which can be evidenced by browsing any menu in any country and noticing how frequently potatoes are a major feature of a dish: from French fries, Swiss potato rösti and Italian potato gnocchi to Irish colcannon and Spanish omelette.

Bake them, boil them, roast them or deep-fry them, potatoes seem the most adaptable and undemanding of vegetables.

Potatoes should be clean, firm and smooth. Avoid potatoes that are wrinkled, have wilted skins, soft dark areas or a green appearance. Choose potatoes with uniform shape and size so that there won't be too much waste in peeling and so that they will cook evenly.

BASIC RECIPE 50

Potato Purée and Variations

Makes 500 g

For potato purée, bake the potatoes rather than boil them. By cooking this way, the potatoes do not absorb any moisture during the cooking process, allowing more cream and butter to be incorporated into them, which results in a smoother and creamier potato purée.

600 g	**large potatoes**
70 ml	**fresh cream**
70 ml	**milk**
50 g	**unsalted butter, diced**
	salt
	freshly ground pepper

Preheat the oven to 180 °C. Scrub the potatoes under cold running water and place on a baking tray. Bake in the oven for 70–90 minutes, depending on their size. Check the potatoes with the tip of a knife to make sure that they are cooked through. Remove the potatoes from the oven and cut them in half. Using a large spoon, scoop out the flesh and discard the skins. Pass the potato through a drum sieve over a large bowl.

Bring the cream and milk to the boil and work it into the potato. Add the butter, piece by piece, until fully incorporated into the potato. Season to taste with salt and freshly ground pepper.

VARIATIONS OF POTATO PURÉE

Garlic Potato Purée: Follow the Potato Purée recipe and add 2 cloves crushed garlic to the milk and cream as you bring it to the boil. Remove from the heat once boiled and allow to infuse for 10 minutes. Pass the milk and cream through a fine sieve to remove the garlic before adding to the potatoes.

Truffle Potato Purée: Add finely chopped truffle and truffle oil to taste to the basic Potato Purée.

Horseradish Potato Purée: Add either horseradish cream or freshly grated horseradish to taste to the basic Potato Purée.

BASIC RECIPE 51

Crushed Potatoes and Variations

Makes 4 portions

500 g	baby potatoes, skin on
50 ml	extra virgin olive oil
	salt
	freshly ground pepper
	lemon juice
15 ml	sliced chives

Scrub the potatoes under cold running water. Place them in a steamer and steam for 15–20 minutes, depending on their size, until tender. Remove from the steamer and, when cool enough to handle, peel them.

Warm the olive oil over a low heat in a heavy-based saucepan and add the potatoes, crushing them with a fork into small chunky pieces. Season with salt, freshly ground pepper and a squeeze of fresh lemon juice. Remove from the heat when warmed through and cover with clingfilm until ready to serve. Just before serving, fold through the sliced chives.

VARIATIONS

Celery Crushed Potatoes: Follow the Crushed Potatoes recipe, but omit the chives and add 100 g peeled, thinly sliced and blanched celery and warm through.

Olive Crushed Potatoes: Follow the Crushed Potatoes recipe, but omit the chives and add 75–100 g tapenade (*Basic Recipe 37, page 74*) or pitted black olives and warm through.

Pesto Crushed Potatoes: Follow the Crushed Potatoes recipe, but omit the chives and add 75–100 g pesto and warm through.

Saffron Crushed Potatoes: Follow the Crushed Potatoes recipe, but omit the chives. Add a pinch of saffron threads as you warm the oil and allow them to bleed a little before adding the potatoes.

Herbed Crushed Potatoes: Follow the Crushed Potatoes recipe. Add 30 ml chopped herbs of your choice, such as chive, parsley, mint, basil, coriander or tarragon and warm through.

Colcannon

Makes 600 g

12	slices pancetta
400 g	Potato Purée (*Basic Recipe 50, page 217*)
120 g	savoy cabbage, stalks removed, chopped and blanched
60 g	spring onions, sliced
1	shallot, peeled and sliced
	salt
	freshly ground pepper
15 ml	chopped flat-leaf parsley

Preheat the oven to 180 °C. Lay the sliced pancetta on a tray and cook in the oven for 4–5 minutes until crisp. Remove from the tray and drain on kitchen paper to absorb any excess fat. Break up the pancetta into small pieces.

Place the potato purée in a heavy-based saucepan over a gentle heat and add the savoy cabbage, spring onions, shallot and pancetta and warm through. Season to taste with salt and freshly ground pepper. Just before serving, fold the parsley through the colcannon.

PRAWN COLCANNON

As a variation, cooked, diced prawns may be added to make prawn colcannon to serve with any fried or roasted fish dish.

Baby Potatoes Roasted in Duck Fat

Serves 4

160 g	baby potatoes
40 ml	rendered duck fat (*Basic Technique 12, page 168*)
2	cloves garlic, crushed
2	sprigs fresh thyme
	salt
	freshly ground pepper
25 g	unsalted butter

Scrub the skins of the potatoes under cold running water, and then cook in salted water over medium heat until tender. When cooked, allow to cool before peeling. Refrigerate until ready to use.

Heat the rendered duck fat in a large cast-iron pan and add the potatoes, garlic and thyme. Season with salt and freshly ground pepper and fry the potatoes for 8–10 minutes, tossing frequently until tender and golden brown. Add the butter and continue to cook for a further 2 minutes. Drain the potatoes and remove the garlic and thyme. (Pass the excess fat through a fine sieve. Keep refrigerated as it can be used again.) Check the seasoning and adjust if necessary. The potatoes can be fried in advance and reheated in a little rendered duck fat before serving.

Potato Dauphinoise

Serves 8

250 ml	fresh cream
3	cloves garlic, peeled and crushed
3	sprigs fresh thyme
20 ml	Clarified Butter (*Basic Recipe 10, page 39*)
6	large potatoes, peeled
	salt
	freshly ground pepper
50 g	Gruyère cheese, grated

Preheat the oven to 180 °C. Heat the cream, garlic and thyme in a saucepan and simmer over low heat for 5 minutes. Remove from the stove and allow to infuse while you prepare the potatoes.

Line a small rectangular roasting tray or baking pan (20 x 15 x 4 cm) with greaseproof paper. Brush the sides of the tray with clarified butter. Slice the potatoes as thin as possible.

Pass the cream through a fine sieve and discard the garlic and thyme. Arrange a layer of potato slices on the bottom of the tray. Season with salt and freshly ground pepper. Sprinkle with a little cheese and drizzle a little of the cream over the potatoes. Continue layering to the top of the tray, pressing each layer down to eliminate any gaps or air pockets. Reserve a little of the cheese.

Cover the tray with aluminium foil and bake for 45 minutes until the potatoes are cooked through. Remove the foil and increase the oven temperature to 220 °C. Sprinkle the remaining cheese over the top of the potatoes and bake until crisp and golden brown.

Sautéed Potatoes

Makes 4 portions

2	large potatoes, washed
100 ml	Clarified Butter (*Basic Recipe 10, page 39*)
1	clove garlic, crushed
1	sprig fresh thyme
	salt
	freshly ground pepper
25 g	unsalted butter

Peel the potatoes, trim into even blocks and cut into 5 mm cubes. Place the potatoes in a container and run cold water over them for 5 minutes. Drain and dry the potatoes on a clean tea towel.

Heat the clarified butter in a large cast-iron pan and add the potatoes, garlic and thyme. Season with salt and freshly ground pepper and fry the potatoes for 8–10 minutes. Toss frequently until tender and golden brown. Add the unsalted butter and continue to cook for a further 2 minutes. Drain the potatoes and remove the garlic and thyme. Check the seasoning and adjust if necessary. The potatoes can be fried in advanced and reheated in a little clarified butter before serving.

BASIC RECIPE 52

Rösti Potatoes

Makes 4 portions

850 g	large potatoes, washed
100 ml	Clarified Butter (*Basic Recipe 10, page 39*)
50 g	onions, sliced
100 g	bacon, julienned
	salt
	freshly ground pepper

Boil the potatoes in their skins in salted water until they are cooked three-quarters of the way through, remaining slightly firm. This is important as they are going to be grated and re-cooked a second time. Remove the potatoes from the water and allow to cool in the fridge before peeling.

Heat 20 ml clarified butter in a pan, add the onions and bacon and sweat without colour. Remove from the pan and allow to cool. Grate the potato on the largest blade of the grater to create long strips.

Preheat the oven to 180 °C. Gently mix the onions and bacon through the potato and season with salt and freshly ground pepper. To make individual rösti, form the potatoes into balls weighing 200 g each. Make the rösti in individual blini pans. Heat 10 ml clarified butter in each of the blini pans and add a ball of potato to each one. Using a palette knife, press the potatoes down so that they have an even, flat surface. Run the palette knife around the sides of the pans to prevent the rösti from sticking.

Over a gentle heat, cook the rösti for 6–7 minutes until they are crisp and golden brown. Turn out the rösti onto a plate. Wipe out the pans. Add another 10 ml clarified butter to the pans and cook the other side of the rösti until crisp and golden brown. Transfer the rösti to the oven and cook for a further 5 minutes to make sure that they are heated through. The rösti can be prepared in advance and reheated in the oven before serving.

Tortilla

Serves 6

1 kg	floury potatoes, peeled and cut into paper-thin slices
1	onion, peeled and finely chopped
1	clove garlic, peeled and finely chopped
4	sprigs fresh thyme
1 L	olive oil
	salt
	freshly ground pepper
8	free-range eggs

Place the potatoes, onion, garlic and thyme in a heavy-based saucepan. Cover with 950 ml of the olive oil and lightly season with salt and freshly ground pepper. Place over a medium heat until the oil just starts to warm, reduce the heat to low and gently cook the potatoes until they are completely cooked and soft (30–35 minutes).

Empty the potatoes into a chinois and allow all of the oil to drain off. The oil can be strained and used again another two or three times.

Whisk the eggs and season lightly with salt and freshly ground pepper. Reserve 150 ml of the egg mixture in a separate bowl. Add the potato to the remaining egg and gently mix so that the potato is evenly coated with egg.

Heat enough olive oil to cover the base of a 28 cm non-stick frying pan over medium heat. Pour in the tortilla mix. As the mixture begins to set, shake the pan in a circular motion to ensure even cooking. Using a wooden spatula, shape the tortilla into a thick disc shape. Cook for a further 2 minutes, then cover the pan with a large, flat plate and flip the tortilla onto the plate. Gently slide the tortilla back into the pan, uncooked-side down, and reduce the heat to low.

Smooth out any imperfections on the cooked surface of the tortilla by pouring a little of the reserved beaten egg over and smoothing it with a wooden spoon. Continue to cook for 2 minutes. Flip the tortilla again and repeat the smoothing process, cover and cook for a further 2 minutes. Repeat the process again and cook for another 2 minutes.

When done the tortilla should not be completely firm, but should have a little wobble in it when you gently shake the pan. Remove from the heat and keep in a warm place for 5 minutes. Transfer it onto a plate and cover with clingfilm for 5 minutes to allow the residual heat to set the remaining uncooked egg.

Serve the tortilla whole or cut into wedges. It is good served either hot or at room temperature, but not chilled.

DESSERT AND PASTRY

The dessert course is as important as the preceding courses and most chefs prefer that they be served individually, assembled on the plate. All the basic preparation is done in advance, but the desserts are only finished and put together in the kitchen on order, meaning they are always fresh and delicate.

The pastry kitchen is a little more complex than the hot and cold kitchen and recipes and methods are a lot more scientific. Like the hot kitchen, many of the basic parts of the finished dish can be made in advance, such as sugar syrups, custards, batters, doughs, macerated fruits, churned ice creams and sorbets and sauces, allowing for more time to focus on the main ingredient, preparation and assembly. As with the hot kitchen, I dislike mixing too many flavours – the look and taste of the main ingredient of the dessert must be paramount. Chocolate, berries, stone fruit, citrus fruits and vanilla are some of the most common and versatile ingredients used on the dessert menu.

Chocolate

Chocolate comes in a variety of flavours, colours and qualities and can be turned into an endless selection of desserts – either hot or cold – from baked chocolate tart, truffles, petits fours, ice creams and sorbets, mousse, parfait and cookies to rich sauces. It is also used in the savoury kitchen to thicken and add a slight bitterness to game sauces or, in countries such as Mexico, it is used in dishes such as *mole*.

Chocolate is widely available in many grades and price varies dramatically depending on the quality of the beans and how they are handled. The amount of cocoa butter, sugar, vanilla and many other ingredients that can be added to chocolate will determine the quality of the final product.

Chocolate can be paired with an affinity of flavours such as nuts, citrus fruit, liquors, herbs, fruit and coffee. For best results use chocolate with a 60%, or higher, cocoa butter content to prevent the flavour being diluted once other ingredients or flavourings are added to the chocolate, such as cream, eggs, butter or fragrant alcohol. Callebaut, Lindt, Valrhona, Felchlin, Café-Tasse, Belfine and Dolfin are all good brands to use with varying cocoa butter levels. When choosing cocoa powder, buy it from the same manufacturer to ensure quality, as it will have been produced from the residue of the chocolate liquor.

To melt chocolate, grate or chop it into small pieces, place into a bowl and melt over a double boiler, taking care to prevent any contact with moisture, which would seize the chocolate and render it unusable. Never melt chocolate over direct heat as it burns easily.

Chocolate should be stored in a cool, dry environment in a sealed container and, depending on the quality of the chocolate and how it is stored, it will have a shelf life of several months and up to two years, even when opened.

Berries

The dessert menu comes to life from late spring through to late summer with the arrival of all the different berries, stone fruit and soft fruit such as figs. When berries are at their ripest it is best to enjoy them whole for maximum flavour and taste, serving them with a flavoured cream, a light syrup, a crisp pastry or a delicate curd or vanilla-scented blanc mange. Take care to use light, delicate flavours that will not overpower the berries.

Choose plump, bright, unblemished berries. Avoid any that are white around the stalk as they are underripe and will be hard, dry and tasteless. Once picked, the softer berries such as raspberries, white and red currants, wild alpine strawberries, blackberries and mulberries will deteriorate quickly. They should be removed from their punnets and kept uncovered in the fridge on a tray lined with a clean cloth.

If the berries need to be washed, plunge them quickly into cold water before they are hulled to prevent any water from getting into the fruit and then place on a clean tea towel to absorb any excess water. Check the insides of raspberries for tiny maggots that often burrow into them but, if possible, avoid washing them.

Overripe and slightly blemished fruit bought cheaply is worth the investment in time sorting through them, as they can be turned into various inexpensive desserts. Once picked through and trimmed they can be puréed and used in sorbets, ice creams or bavarois. Cooked in a double boiler over very low heat with a sprinkling of sugar, the berries will release all their juices, which may be passed off, chilled and served as a consommé with a selection of freshly sliced summer fruit (*page 271*), particularly white peaches served with a creamy sorbet such as mascarpone or fromage blanc. Blackberries steeped in brandy, sugar and white wine vinegar can be turned into beautifully sharp and intense vinegar and, with the addition of nut oils, mustard and seasoning, transformed into a dressing to be served with warm game salads.

Citrus fruits

Citrus plays a big role in the pastry kitchen. A dessert or tangy sorbet made from citrus fruit such as pink grapefruit, blood orange or lime is a refreshing and light way to end a meal.

Before using the zest, remove the pith, which is very bitter. Use a swivel peeler to yield wide strips of peel and use the tip of a knife to remove the layer of white pith. The zest can be infused into syrups and Crème Anglaise (*page 232*) to make citrus-flavoured custards, curds, bavarois, crème brûlée and ice creams.

Blanch in several changes of water to remove the bitterness of the zest and cook in sugar syrup (*Basic Recipe 53, page 229*). Then dip into either sugar or chocolate to make delicious, inexpensive petits fours. Grate into tuile mixes or batter to make orange tuiles or lemon financiers.

Vanilla

Vanilla is an essential ingredient in the pastry kitchen. It is obtained from the bean or pod of the wild orchid *Vanilla planifolia*. Grown in the tropics, the finest vanilla comes from Madagascar, Tahiti, Mexico and the West Indies. The beans are picked and dried in the sun, which leaves them dark and shrivelled.

When buying vanilla pods, they should feel moist and have a strong perfume. Vanilla pods should be stored in a sealed container and refrigerated until ready to use. To obtain maximum flavour from the pods, split them lengthways and scrape out the seeds with the tip of a knife (*page 232*).

Vanilla pods can be used 3 or 4 times if washed under cold running water and dried after using, but will gradually lose their flavour. Store the used vanilla pods in a sealed container of castor sugar to make vanilla sugar (*page 227*). The sugar will become perfumed with the vanilla and can be used in pastry recipes that call for sugar or can be used to make vanilla syrup (*page 229*). The syrup can then be used in sorbets, for poaching fruits such as pears (*page 262*), peaches or apricots, or for adding to fruit coulis.

If using vanilla extract, use a pure vanilla extract made from macerated vanilla pods. Avoid those that have been chemically enhanced as they have a very harsh flavour. A small drop of pure vanilla essence will go a long way as it has a very intense flavour and should be used sparingly.

OTHER INGREDIENTS

It is essential to use only extremely fresh, top-quality ingredients: eggs must be fresh and come from a reliable source; cream should always be fresh and pasteurised to avoid the spread of any bacteria; and, unless otherwise specified, always use unsalted butter, castor sugar and sifted cake flour.

PRACTICAL ADVICE BEFORE STARTING PASTRY RECIPES

- Have all the equipment needed for the recipe ready to hand.
- Weigh out and measure all the ingredients before you begin and keep them in separate containers.
- Preheat the oven to the necessary temperature.
- To ensure that egg whites rise perfectly, use scrupulously clean utensils rinsed in cold water and dried. Make sure the egg whites contain no trace of yolk.

Sugar and Syrups

Sugar syrup or stock syrup is a dessert basic and is good for dressing fruits or as a liquid in which to poach them. Basic sugar syrup can be flavoured in numerous ways with the addition of split vanilla pods, star anise, cinnamon sticks, sliced fresh ginger, cardamom, lemon grass, citrus peel, fresh lime, espresso, basil or mint.

Vanilla Sugar

Makes 250 g

2	**pods vanilla**
250 g	**castor sugar**

Vanilla pods can be used more than once. Rinse off under cold water and dry. Place the pods into an airtight jar with the castor sugar and leave to infuse for 2 days before using. Use in pastry recipes that call for sugar in cakes, puddings, custards and creams.

BASIC RECIPE 53

Sugar Syrup and Flavoured Sugar Syrup

Makes 100 ml

100 g castor sugar
100 ml water

Mix the sugar and water together in a heavy-based saucepan. Place over medium heat and stir until the sugar has dissolved. Bring to the boil, reduce the heat and continue to cook for 3 minutes, skimming off any scum that floats to the surface. Pass through a fine sieve into a clean bowl and allow to cool. Store in a sealed container in the fridge for up to 1 month.

VANILLA SYRUP

Add 1 split vanilla pod to the recipe above and allow to infuse in the syrup for 3 hours before using.

Lime Syrup

Makes 500 ml

200 g castor sugar
300 ml water
juice of 3 limes
grated zest of 6 limes

Mix everything together in a heavy-based saucepan. Place over medium heat and stir until the sugar has dissolved. Bring to the boil, reduce the heat and continue to cook for 3 minutes, skimming off any scum that floats to the surface. Transfer the syrup into a clean bowl and allow to cool, leaving the lime zest in the syrup to infuse and impart its flavour into the syrup. Store in a sealed container in the fridge. Pass the syrup through a fine sieve when ready to use and discard the zest.

Coffee Syrup

Makes 450 ml

350 ml Sugar Syrup (*Basic Recipe 53, page 229)*
100 ml strong espresso coffee

Place the sugar syrup and coffee together in a heavy-based saucepan and bring to the boil. Reduce the heat and simmer for 5 minutes. Pass the syrup through a fine chinois and refrigerate until ready to use.

Pistachio Syrup

Makes 550 ml

500 ml Sugar Syrup (*Basic Recipe 53, page 229*)
50 g pistachio paste

Bring the sugar syrup to the boil in a heavy-based saucepan and whisk in the pistachio paste. Bring back to the boil and reduce the heat to the lowest possible setting. Cook for 15 minutes. Remove the pistachio syrup from the heat and stand in a warm place for 2 hours. Pass through a fine sieve and refrigerate until ready to use.

BASIC RECIPE 54

Praline

Makes 150 g

Praline is made from a combination of nuts – usually skinned almonds or hazelnuts, either whole or ground into a powder – and caramel. Praline can also be used to describe chocolate confection containing powdered or whole nuts. Praline can be added to ice cream, can be used to coat chocolate truffles (*page 257*), or can be coated in a thin layer of chocolate and used for petits fours. It can also be used as a crunchy base to a chocolate tart or cheesecake. If not using immediately, store in an airtight jar.

65 g	**sugar**
65 ml	**water**
50 g	**hazelnuts**
50 g	**nibbed almonds**

Brush a stainless steel tray with a thin layer of vegetable oil. Set aside until ready to use.

Put the sugar and water in a heavy-based saucepan and set over low heat until the sugar has completely melted and is beginning to boil. Wash down the inside of the pan with a pastry brush dipped in cold water to prevent any crystals from forming. Cook the sugar until it turns a deep amber colour. Add the hazelnuts and almonds and continue to cook gently until the caramel becomes liquid again. Pour out onto the oiled tray and allow to cool. Remove the praline from the tray and chop finely, almost to a powder.

Chocolate Praline

Makes 350 g

This can be used as a base for cheesecakes or chocolate truffle cake. It can also be cut into shapes and served as a petit four, or chopped finely and sprinkled over desserts as a garnish.

150 g	**Praline (*Basic Recipe 54, see above*)**
125 g	**dark chocolate, chopped**

Make the praline as in the recipe above and chop finely, almost to a powder.

Melt the chocolate over a double boiler. Add the praline and mix through the chocolate until evenly distributed. Pour the chocolate praline onto a tray lined with greaseproof paper and allow to set in the fridge before using.

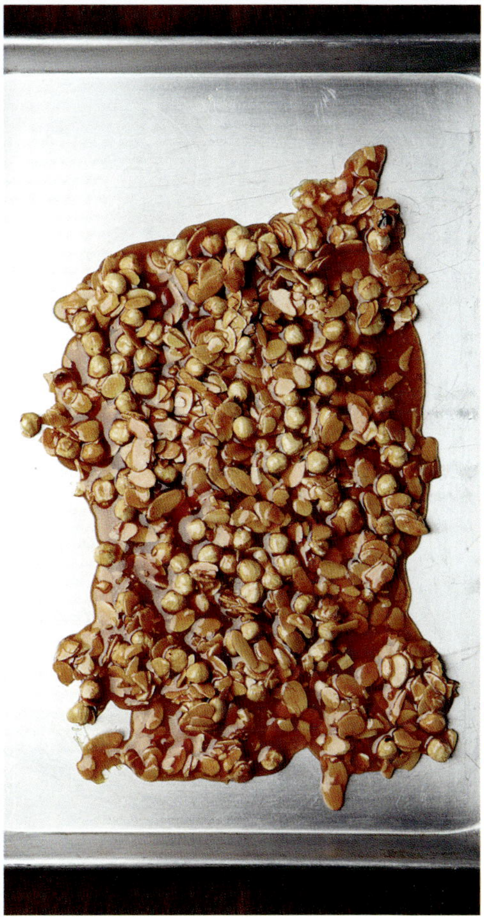

BASIC RECIPE 55

Crème Anglaise

Makes 400 ml

Crème anglaise is the base for both ice cream and sweet sauces and can be infused with different ingredients for an endless range of flavours.

½	pod vanilla
250 ml	milk
3	free-range egg yolks
65 g	castor sugar

Split the vanilla pod and scrape out the seeds using the tip of a knife. Bring the milk, vanilla pod and seeds to the boil in a heavy-based saucepan. Remove from the heat and allow the vanilla to infuse for 15 minutes.

Beat the egg yolks and sugar in a bowl until pale, doubled in volume and the sugar has dissolved. Pour half the milk into the egg yolk mix and whisk together. Pour the mixture back into the saucepan with the remaining milk and whisk. Cook the crème anglaise over very low heat, stirring continuously until it thickens. It is ready when it coats the back of a spoon and your finger leaves a clear path when run through the crème. Remove the saucepan from the heat and pass the crème through a fine sieve into a clean bowl. Set the bowl over a larger bowl filled with ice to cool the crème anglaise as quickly as possible. Stir from time to time to prevent a skin from forming.

BASIC RECIPE 56

Crème Pâtissière

Makes 750 ml

Similar to crème anglaise, but with the addition of flour, crème pâtissière can also be flavoured with the addition of alcohol, chocolate or flavoured pastes. It is used as a filling for pastries, gâteaux and petits fours.

6	free-range egg yolks
125 g	castor sugar
40 g	plain flour
500 ml	milk
1	pod vanilla, split lengthways
	a little icing sugar or butter

Whisk the egg yolks and one-third of the sugar together in a bowl to a light ribbon consistency. Whisk in the flour thoroughly.

Heat the milk with the rest of the sugar and the vanilla pod in a heavy-based saucepan over medium heat. As soon as it comes to the boil, pour it into the egg yolk mixture, stirring as you go. Mix well, and return the mixture to the pan. Bring to the boil over a medium heat, whisking continuously. Let it bubble for 2 minutes and then pour into a bowl.

Dust the crème pâtissière with a veil of icing sugar to prevent a skin forming as it cools, or dot small flakes of butter all over the surface. Once cold, it can be kept in the fridge for up to 3 days. Remove the vanilla pod before using.

Pistachio Crème Pâtissière

Makes 900 ml

1	pod vanilla
500 ml	milk
60 g	pistachio paste
6	free-range egg yolks
125 g	castor sugar
40 g	plain flour, sifted
5 ml	icing sugar

Split the vanilla pod and scrape out the seeds using the tip of a knife. Bring the milk, vanilla pod and seeds to the boil in a heavy-based saucepan and whisk in the pistachio paste. Bring back to the boil over a gentle heat.

Beat the egg yolks and sugar in a bowl until pale, doubled in volume and the sugar has dissolved. Beat the flour into the egg mix. Pour the boiled milk into the egg mix and whisk until fully incorporated. Pour into a clean saucepan and return to a low heat, stirring continuously with a wooden spoon until thick. Transfer the pistachio crème pâtissière into a clean bowl and dust with icing sugar to prevent a skin from forming on the surface. Cover with clingfilm when cool and refrigerate until ready to use. It will keep for up to 3 days.

BASIC RECIPE 57

Raspberry Coulis

Makes 250 ml

Fruit coulis are easy sweet sauces to make and go well with all types of desserts, from ice cream to tarts. Most fruits are suitable for making coulis and can be flavoured and infused with alcohol, herbs and spices.

400 g	raspberries
50 ml	Sugar Syrup (*Basic Recipe 53, page 229*)
	icing sugar
	lemon juice

Cook the raspberries and sugar syrup in a heavy-based saucepan for 5 minutes over low heat. Transfer to a food processor and blend to a purée, then strain through a fine sieve. Add icing sugar and a squeeze of lemon juice to taste. Thin with a little mineral water if the purée is too thick. Refrigerate the raspberry coulis until ready to use. It will keep for 2–3 days.

Strawberry Coulis

Makes 250 ml

400 g	strawberries, hulled and chopped
50 ml	Sugar Syrup (*Basic Recipe 53, page 229*)
	icing sugar
	lemon juice

Cook the strawberries and sugar syrup in a heavy-based saucepan for 5 minutes over low heat. Transfer to a food processor and blend to a purée, then strain through a fine sieve. Add icing sugar and a squeeze of lemon juice to taste. Thin with a little mineral water if the purée is too thick. Refrigerate the strawberry coulis until ready to use. It will keep for 2–3 days.

Blackberry Coulis

Makes 300 ml

300 g	blackberries
50 ml	Sugar Syrup (*Basic Recipe 53, page 229*)
	icing sugar
	lemon juice

Cook the blackberries and sugar syrup in a heavy-based saucepan for 5 minutes over low heat. Transfer to a food processor and blend to a purée, then strain through a fine sieve. Add icing sugar and a squeeze of lemon juice to taste. Thin with a little mineral water if the purée is too thick. Refrigerate the blackberry coulis until ready to use. It will keep for 2–3 days.

Mango Coulis

Makes 400 ml

2	medium, ripe mangoes, peeled, pipped and chopped
100 g	icing sugar
100 ml	water
	lemon juice

Mix the mango, sugar and water together in a heavy-based saucepan and cook over low heat for 5 minutes. Transfer to a food processor and blend to a purée, then strain through a fine sieve. Add lemon juice to taste.

BASIC RECIPE 58

Chocolate Sauce

Makes 250 ml

This sauce can be made in advance and refrigerated until ready to use. If the chocolate sauce solidifies, simply reheat it in a bowl over a pot of simmering water until it is liquid again. The sauce can be flavoured with the addition of alcohol, such as crème de menthe, whiskey, brandy or liqueurs such as Baileys.

150 ml	milk
50 ml	fresh cream
30 g	castor sugar
250 g	dark chocolate, at least 60% cocoa solids, chopped
30 g	unsalted butter, diced

Bring the milk, cream and sugar to the boil in a heavy-based saucepan over medium heat. Remove from the heat and allow to cool slightly. Add the chopped chocolate and stir over low heat until melted. Whisk in the diced butter and, when fully incorporated, pass through a fine sieve.

BASIC RECIPE 59

Vanilla Bean Ice Cream

Makes 550 ml approximately

1	pod vanilla
250 ml	milk
250 ml	fresh cream
6	free-range egg yolks
85 g	castor sugar

Split the vanilla pod lengthways and scrape out the seeds using the tip of a knife. In a heavy-based saucepan over medium heat, bring the milk, cream, vanilla pod and seeds to the boil. Remove from the heat and allow the vanilla to infuse the milk for 15 minutes.

Whisk the egg yolks and sugar together in a large bowl until pale, doubled in volume and the sugar has dissolved.

Return the vanilla-infused milk to the heat and bring back to the boil. Remove from the heat and pour half of the milk into the egg yolk mix, whisking together until well blended. Add the remaining milk and whisk until well blended.

Pour the custard mixture into a clean saucepan and cook over low heat for 8–10 minutes until it thickens, stirring continuously with a wooden spoon. To test if the custard is ready, run your finger over the back of the wooden spoon: if the custard leaves a definite parting, it is ready; if it is still runny, it will need a few more minutes of cooking. The custard can also be checked with a sugar thermometer and is ready when it has a reading of 82 °C/175 °F. Do not allow the custard to boil or it will curdle.

Strain the mixture through a fine sieve into a clean bowl. Place this over a bowl of ice and stir to cool the custard as quickly as possible. Stir from time to time to prevent a skin from forming.

Pour into an electric ice-cream maker and churn until firm. Remove from the machine, transfer to a clean container and freeze for up to a week until ready to serve. Allow the ice cream to soften slightly at room temperature before serving.

VARIATIONS OF VANILLA BEAN ICE CREAM

Citrus-flavoured ice cream: Infuse the crème anglaise base with citrus peel, pass and finish with a dash of an appropriate flavoured alcohol, such as Grand Marnier for an orange-flavoured ice cream.

Coffee ice cream: Add a shot of strong espresso coffee and a dash of coffee liqueur to taste.

Ginger ice cream: Infuse the milk with fresh, peeled root ginger, pass and finish with chopped preserved ginger in verjuice.

Balsamic ice cream: Flavour the crème anglaise base with good quality balsamic and serve with fresh strawberries.

Basil, lemon thyme or mint ice cream: Infuse the crème anglaise base with chopped fresh basil, lemon thyme or mint. Pass through a fine sieve before churning and discard the herbs.

Coconut ice cream: Replace the milk with coconut milk and cream with coconut cream and follow the same method. Finish with a dash of appropriate alcohol, such as Malibu.

Praline ice cream: Add chopped praline (*Basic Recipe 54, page 230*) to the finished churned ice cream.

Picture on next page

BASIC RECIPE 60

Basic Yeast Dough

Makes 500 g

This is a great, quick and easy dough, perfect for making the classic Provençal snack, pissaladière (the French equivalent of pizza). Vary the toppings: sun-dried tomatoes and olives, rosemary and red onions, artichokes and anchovies.

5 ml	**fresh yeast**
185 ml	**water**
310 g	**strong white bread flour**
5 ml	**salt**

Before you start, make sure all the ingredients are at room temperature. In a small bowl, whisk together the fresh yeast and water until completely dissolved.

Put all the ingredients into an electric mixer fitted with a dough hook. Knead on the lowest speed for 4 minutes. Make sure the flour is mixed in completely and then increase the speed to medium. Continue kneading for a further 4 minutes, or until the dough is soft and silky. Cover the bowl with a cloth and leave in a warm place for about 30 minutes to prove.

When ready to bake, preheat the oven to 180 °C. Scoop the dough out onto a lightly floured work surface and roll out a circle or rectangle about 1 cm thick. Carefully transfer to a greased baking tray. Refrigerate for 10 minutes to rest, then top with the ingredients of your choice and bake for 12–15 minutes.

Pissaladière

Serves 4

100 g	**Lyonnaise Onions (*Basic Recipe 43, page 194*)**
50 g	**anchovy fillets, halved lengthways**
12	**black olives, pitted and halved**
	olive oil

Spread the onions onto the prepared dough (above) in a thick layer. Arrange the anchovy strips across the surface to form a diamond pattern and stud each diamond with an olive. Drizzle with olive oil and bake for 20 minutes at 180 °C until the base is crisp and golden brown.

BASIC RECIPE 61

Rough Puff Pastry

Makes 1 kg

500 g	**strong white bread flour, plus extra for dusting**
5 ml	**salt**
500 g	**chilled unsalted butter, cut into 1 cm dice**
250 ml	**iced water**

Sift the flour and salt into a large mixing bowl. Rub the cold butter roughly into the flour until the mixture resembles lumpy, coarse breadcrumbs. Work quickly to prevent the butter from getting too warm. Add the iced water and bring the mix together. On a heavily floured work surface and using a rolling pin, work the dough into a rectangle, approximately 40 x 25 cm. Use the side of the rolling pin to knock the edges of the rectangle into as neat a shape as possible. Brush off any excess flour with a pastry brush and rest the pastry in the fridge for 30 minutes.

Return the pastry to a lightly floured work surface. Bring both ends of the rectangle into the middle, and then fold over like a book to create four layers of pastry. Turn the rectangle through 90 degrees so the shorter edge is facing you. Repeat the rolling and folding process four times, resting the pastry for 30 minutes between each fold. Place the pastry back in the fridge for 1 hour before using.

BASIC RECIPE 62

Blinis

Makes 500 ml

Leavening

250 ml	**lukewarm milk**
15 g	**fresh yeast**
25 g	**plain or wholemeal flour**

Batter

125 g	**plain or wholemeal flour**
2	**free-range eggs, separated**
	salt

LEAVENING

In a bowl, whisk together the lukewarm milk and yeast and then add the flour. Cover the bowl with a plate and leave at room temperature (24 °C) for 2 hours.

BATTER

Using a spatula, stir the flour and egg yolks into the leavening. Cover with a plate and leave at room temperature for 1 hour.

Place the egg whites in a bowl, beat well, then add a pinch of salt and beat until stiff. Fold them carefully into the batter.

The batter is now ready to use. Use the batter as soon as possible and certainly within an hour, or it will ferment and the flavour will be spoilt.

To cook the blinis, heat 5 ml Clarified Butter (*Basic Recipe 10, page 39*) in a heavy-based frying pan over medium heat. Add the blini batter, making the blini as big or as small as required. Cook for 1–1½ minutes, depending on the thickness of the blini, until golden brown. Turn the blini over and cook the other side. Transfer the blini from the frying pan to a wire rack.

Cherry and Almond Clafoutis

Serves 6

Based on the classic French favourite, here an almond-flavoured batter is baked in a shallow pan over a layer of pitted fresh cherries. Prepare the batter and fruits in advance, but put them together and bake the pudding at the last minute. The batter benefits from resting for a full 24 hours. You can either make one large pudding or 6 small ones. Classically made with black cherries, clafoutis can be made with other fruits such as plums, apples, pears or berries. It is then called flaugnarde.

50 g	**ground almonds**
15 g	**strong plain flour**
	sea salt
100 g	**castor sugar**
2	**large free-range eggs**
3	**large free-range egg yolks**
250 ml	**double cream**
300 g	**ripe fresh cherries, or**
	250 g marinated cherries, drained
	unsalted butter, softened, for greasing pan
	icing sugar, sifted, for dusting

Put the ground almonds, flour, a good pinch of sea salt and the sugar into the food processor and whizz for a few seconds to blend. Add the eggs, egg yolks and cream and blend to a smooth batter, scraping down the sides of the bowl once or twice. Tip into a jug or bowl, cover and refrigerate for 24 hours.

In the meantime, pit the cherries and pat them dry if they are particularly juicy. Rub the inside of a large ovenproof sauté pan or gratin dish, 23–25 cm in diameter, with softened butter.

Preheat the oven to 190 °C. Scatter the cherries over the base of the pan or dish. Stir the batter in the jug and pour over the cherries. Bake for about 20 minutes, or until risen and golden brown. The middle may be slightly flatter than the surrounding batter but it should be set. If not, then bake a little longer.

Dust with icing sugar and serve at once.

TO MAKE INDIVIDUAL CLAFOUTIS

Butter 6 tartlet tins or Yorkshire pudding tins, 10 cm in diameter, and divide the cherries between them. Pour in the batter and bake at 200 °C for 10–12 minutes.

pat. pend.
Design AG. Switzerland

Doughnuts with Hot Chocolate Sauce

Serves 6

Doughnuts

250 g	**plain flour, sifted, plus extra for dusting**
5 ml	**salt**
25 g	**castor sugar**
15 g	**fresh yeast**
40 ml	**full-cream milk**
1	**large free-range egg, lightly beaten**
40 g	**diced, soft unsalted butter**
	canola oil for deep-frying

Cinnamon Sugar

100 g	**castor sugar**
5 ml	**ground cinnamon**

100 ml **Chocolate Sauce (*Basic Recipe 58, page 236*)**

DOUGHNUTS

Place the flour, salt and sugar in an electric mixer fitted with a dough hook. Mix slowly until the ingredients are thoroughly blended. Crumble the yeast into the milk and crush it with the back of a spoon to dissolve. Pour the yeast into the mixture and continue to mix. Add the egg, increase the speed of the mixer and continue to mix until the dough comes together in a ball and cleans the sides of the mixing bowl. Add the butter, piece by piece, until fully incorporated. Check the consistency of the dough: if it seems too wet, add a little more flour.

Transfer the dough to a lightly oiled bowl, cover with clingfilm and place in the fridge to prove overnight, or leave to stand at room temperature for 1½–2 hours until the dough has doubled in size.

Remove the dough from the bowl. Knock back and knead the dough for 4–5 minutes on a lightly floured surface.

Place the dough in a piping bag fitted with a 4 cm plain nozzle and pipe out the dough in lines onto the floured surface. Cut the doughnuts into 3 cm lengths. Place the doughnuts apart on a lightly oiled baking tray and cover with clingfilm that has been sprayed with non-stick spray. Place the doughnuts in a warm place and prove for a further 1–2 hours, or until they have doubled in size.

Heat the canola oil to 180 °C in a deep heavy-based pan. Deep-fry the doughnuts, turning them with a slotted spoon until they are evenly golden brown in colour (approximately 1 minute on each side). Remove the doughnuts from the oil and drain on kitchen paper.

CINNAMON SUGAR

Mix the sugar and cinnamon together in a deep bowl. Toss the doughnuts through the cinnamon sugar.

Serve the doughnuts warm with hot chocolate sauce.

Ricotta Hotcakes and Blueberry Compote

Makes 36

225 g	plain flour
12.5 ml	baking powder
2.5 ml	fine salt
2.5 ml	ground cinnamon
60 g	castor sugar
4	large free-range egg yolks
225 g	ricotta cheese
350 ml	milk
90 g	unsalted butter, melted and cooled
5 ml	almond extract
6	large free-range egg whites
	vegetable oil for frying

Sift the flour, baking powder, salt and cinnamon into a large bowl. Stir in the sugar, reserving 15 ml for later.

Whisk the egg yolks in a medium bowl until thickened, then gradually whisk in the ricotta, milk, melted butter and almond extract.

Make a well in the dry ingredients. Slowly pour in the egg yolk mixture, whisking constantly to make a smooth batter.

Put the egg whites in a clean bowl and whisk to soft peaks, adding the reserved sugar halfway through. Fold the egg whites into the ricotta batter.

Heat a large non-stick pan over medium heat. Pour in a little of the oil to cover the bottom of the pan and continue to heat until hot. Spoon the batter into the pan to make four hotcakes, each 8–10 cm in diameter. Cook for 2 minutes until the underside is golden brown, then turn the hotcakes over and cook for another 2 minutes to lightly brown the other side.

Lift the hotcakes out of the pan with a spatula and serve immediately with blueberry compote. Make the remaining hotcakes in the same way.

Blueberry Compote

Makes 250 g

100 ml	Sugar Syrup (*Basic Recipe 53, page 229*)
½	pod vanilla
250 g	blueberries

Bring the sugar syrup and vanilla to the boil in a heavy-based saucepan over medium heat. Add the blueberries and cook for 3 minutes. Remove from the heat and allow to cool. Refrigerate until ready to use.

Caramelised Lemon Tart

Makes 12 portions

Lemon Filling

	grated zest of 4 lemons
265 ml	lemon juice
12	free-range eggs
500 g	castor sugar
400 ml	thickened cream
	icing sugar for dusting

Sweet Pastry

250 g	plain flour
200 g	unsalted butter, diced and softened
100 g	icing sugar
	salt
2	free-range egg yolks
10 g	unsalted butter, softened to line pastry case
	egg wash of 1 free-range egg yolk and 10 ml milk

LEMON FILLING

Wash the lemons, grate the zest, cut the grated lemons in half and squeeze out the juice. Pass the juice through a fine chinois and measure out 265 ml. Break the eggs into a bowl, add the sugar and whisk until smooth and doubled in volume. Stir the lemon juice and grated zest into the egg mix. Whip the cream in a separate bowl to ribbon stage and then whisk it into the egg mix. Refrigerate for 2 hours to allow the lemon zest to infuse before passing through a fine chinois. Discard the zest.

SWEET PASTRY

Sift the flour onto a work surface, make a well in the centre and place the diced butter into it. Sift the icing sugar onto the butter, add a pinch of salt and work it into the butter with your fingertips. Add the egg yolks, gradually draw in the flour, and mix to a smooth dough. Do not overwork the dough. Roll out the dough between 2 sheets of greaseproof paper to flatten; this makes it easier to roll out later. Place in the fridge to rest for 1 hour before using.

Preheat the oven to 170 °C. Brush a 3 cm deep, 21 cm pastry ring with softened butter and refrigerate for 10 minutes. On a lightly floured surface, roll out the pastry to a thickness of 6 mm. Place the pastry ring on a baking tray lined with baking paper and line with the pastry, leaving a little hanging over the sides. Trim off excess pastry. Using a small ball of pastry, press the pastry into the corners of the pastry ring, taking care not to tear the pastry. Rest in the fridge for 10 minutes.

Line the inside of the pastry case with greaseproof paper and fill with baking beans. Blind bake for 15 minutes, then remove from the oven and allow to cool slightly. Remove the beans and greaseproof paper and inspect for any holes or cracks in the pastry. If there are any, fill them with the leftover pastry to prevent the filling from leaking out during cooking. Brush the pastry case with egg wash and return to the oven for a further 5–6 minutes until the pastry is lightly coloured. Remove the pastry case from the oven and brush with the egg wash once more, but do not place back into the oven at this stage. Allow the pastry to cool. Reduce the oven temperature to 140 °C.

Pour in the lemon filling to the top of the pastry case and place back in the oven for 45–50 minutes, until the tart is just set (it will continue to cook in its own heat once removed from the oven). Remove the tart from the oven and leave to cool and set for 4 hours. Do not refrigerate, as the pastry will soften. Using the tip of a sharp knife, trim the edge of the tart of any excess pastry so that the top of the tart is even.

To serve, carefully remove the pastry ring and cut the tart into even-sized slices. Dust each slice generously with icing sugar and glaze with a blowtorch until the sugar melts and begins to caramelise, taking care not to burn the sugar as it will become bitter. For a crisp glaze, dust and glaze the tart a second time.

Pear Tarte Tatin

Serves 6–8

250–300 g	**butter puff pastry or Rough Puff Pastry (*Basic Recipe 61, page 242*)**
	plain flour for dusting
6–8	**firm pears (or apples if you prefer)**
125 g	**cold unsalted butter**
250 g	**castor sugar**

Roll out the puff pastry on a lightly floured surface to a thickness of 3 mm. Flour the pastry lightly and fold up loosely to a manageable shape, cover with clingfilm and rest in the fridge for at least 1 hour before using.

Peel the pears and cut them in half from top to bottom. Remove the stalks and cores. Slice the butter into 2 mm thick slices and completely cover the bottom of a heavy-based 30 cm pan with it. Sprinkle the sugar evenly over the butter. Place the pears, peeled-side down, on top, starting from the outer edge and working into the centre of the pan. The pears need to be packed tightly together. Remove the pastry from the fridge and cut out a disc large enough to cover the entire pan. Lay the pastry over the pears and tuck the excess pastry down the sides so it is tucked in around the pears. Using the tip of a sharp paring knife, make 5 or 6 incisions in the pastry to allow the steam to escape as it bakes.

Preheat the oven to 180 °C. Place the pan on a burner that covers the entire base of the pan. Use a low heat to ensure an even caramelisation of the butter and sugar during cooking. Cook the tarte tatin in this way until an even caramel is reached around the edge of the pan. This can take up to 45 minutes. Transfer the tarte tatin to the oven and cook for a further 40–50 minutes, until the pastry is crisp and golden brown.

Remove the tarte tatin from the oven and allow to rest in the pan for 15 minutes to cool and thicken the caramel. Place a plate or a board large enough to cover the top of the pan over the top of the pan and flip the pan over. The tarte tatin should come away easily. If it is stuck to the pan the caramel has set too much; place it over the burner for 30 seconds to melt the caramel slightly.

Cut the tarte tatin into slices and serve with thick cream or Vanilla Bean Ice Cream (*Basic Recipe 59, page 237*).

Churros and Hot Chocolate

Serves 6

Churros

250 g	plain flour
	salt
50 g	unsalted butter
200 ml	water
	vegetable oil for deep-frying
50 g	castor sugar for dusting

Hot Chocolate

150 g	dark chocolate (70% cocoa solids)
300 ml	double cream
1	pod vanilla, split lengthways
	Baileys Irish Cream or Jameson Whiskey
100 ml	fresh cream

CHURROS

Sift the flour and a pinch of salt into a mixing bowl. Heat the butter and water together in a heavy-based saucepan over medium heat until the butter has melted, then bring to the boil. Add the flour and stir with a wooden spoon until a smooth paste forms. Remove from the heat and transfer to a bowl. Set aside until ready to use.

To cook the churros, heat the oil to 180 °C over medium heat. Spoon the churros mixture into a piping bag fitted with a 2 cm star nozzle. Pipe 10 cm lengths of the mixture directly into the hot oil and deep-fry until golden brown. Remove the churros from the oil with a slotted spoon and place on kitchen paper to drain any excess oil. Dust the churros with castor sugar and serve warm with a glass of the hot chocolate and a spoonful of whipped cream on top of each glass.

HOT CHOCOLATE

Chop the chocolate into small pieces and place in a clean stainless steel bowl. Heat the double cream and split vanilla pod in a heavy-based saucepan over medium heat. Bring to the boil, remove from the heat and allow the vanilla to infuse for 10 minutes before passing the cream through a fine sieve over the chopped chocolate. Add the alcohol to taste. Stir until the chocolate has completely melted. Whisk the cream to ribbon stage.

Pour the hot chocolate into warmed mugs or cups, and spoon the cream on top.

Deep-Fried Chocolate

Makes 500 g

The chocolate ganache must be frozen before deep-frying to prevent it from bursting when dropped into the hot oil. Deep-fry the chocolate in small batches so that the oil maintains its temperature throughout cooking.

420 g	Chocolate Ganache (*page 259*)
75 g	plain flour, sifted
50 g	cocoa powder, sifted
30 ml	cold water
110 ml	warm beer
30 ml	olive oil
1	free-range egg yolk
2	free-range egg whites
	vegetable oil for deep-frying
	icing sugar for dusting
	Chocolate Sauce (*Basic Recipe 58, page 236*), Praline (*Basic Recipe 54, page 230*) and ice cream for serving

Divide the chocolate ganache into 12 x 35 g balls and roll them into neat rounds between the palms of your hands. Insert a long wooden skewer into the centre of each ball. Place the chocolate balls on a tray and freeze them until ready to use.

Prepare the first stage of the batter by whisking together the flour, cocoa, water, warm beer, olive oil and egg yolk to form a smooth batter. Clean down the sides of the bowl and cover with clingfilm to prevent a skin forming. Allow the batter to stand at room temperature for 1 hour.

Heat the oil to 180 °C in a heavy-based saucepan. In a clean bowl, whisk the egg whites until they form peaks and then fold through the batter mixture.

Remove the chocolate balls from the freezer. Dip the chocolate balls into the batter and completely cover each one. Allow any excess batter to drain off. Place 4 chocolate balls into the oil at a time to prevent the oil from dropping temperature and the batter becoming soggy. Cook until the batter crisps, then remove and drain the deep-fried chocolate on kitchen paper. Allow the oil to come back to temperature before deep-frying the next batch and continue to cook until all of the chocolate has been deep-fried.

Remove the deep-fried chocolate from the skewers, dust with icing sugar and place 3 pieces on each plate. Pour a pool of chocolate sauce at one end of the plate. Spoon 10 g of praline between the chocolate sauce and deep-fried chocolate and set a quenelle of ice cream onto the praline. Serve immediately.

Warm Chocolate Fondant

Serves 8

The chocolate fondants can be made in advance and frozen. They can be baked straight from the freezer, but will need an extra few minutes' baking time.

20 g	**unsalted butter, melted, for brushing moulds**
	castor sugar for lining moulds
200 g	**dark chocolate (60% cocoa solids), finely chopped**
200 g	**unsalted butter, softened**
4	**free-range eggs**
4	**free-range egg yolks**
200 g	**icing sugar, sifted, plus extra for dusting**
55 g	**plain flour**
35 g	**cocoa powder**

Preheat the oven to 190 °C. Prepare 8 dariole moulds or ramekins by brushing them well with melted butter, using upwards strokes around the sides. Chill until firm, and then brush again with another layer of butter. Coat the ramekins with sugar, shaking out the excess. Place the ramekins on a baking tray and set aside.

Put the chocolate and softened butter into a stainless steel bowl and set over a pot of simmering water. Stir the chocolate and butter until melted, smooth and fully incorporated. Keep warm.

Using an electric mixer, beat the eggs, egg yolks and icing sugar together until pale and doubled in volume. Reduce the speed of the mixer and add the melted chocolate. Remove the bowl from the mixer and sift in the flour and cocoa powder. Fold them into the chocolate mixture, taking care not to overwork the mixture.

Spoon the mixture evenly between the prepared moulds; they should be just over half-full. Place in the oven and bake for 8–10 minutes. After 8 minutes, remove one of the fondants and check that it is cooked around the edges and the centre still looks soft. Insert a skewer to test the centre – the skewer should come away warm but the centre should remain liquid. If you think it needs more time, return the fondants to the oven for another minute and check again.

Remove the fondants from the oven and rest for 1 minute. Carefully turn out each one onto a serving plate. Dust with icing sugar and serve.

Chocolate Ganache / Chocolate Truffles

Makes 500 ml approximately

Chocolate ganache is the base for chocolate truffles. It is also used as a filling for chocolate truffle cake and to make Deep-Fried Chocolate (*page 256*). Ganache is made from a combination of chocolate (white, milk or dark), cream, butter and alcohol. Once set, the ganache can be piped into long strands and cut into bite-sized pieces or rolled into balls. Dipped in chocolate and rolled in cocoa powder or chopped nuts, they make perfect petits fours to serve with coffee or digestives.

100 ml **fresh cream**
300 g **dark chocolate (60% cocoa solids), chopped**
150 g **unsalted butter, at room temperature**
45 ml **alcohol of your choice (optional)**
cocoa powder for dusting

Bring the cream to the boil in a heavy-based saucepan, then remove from the heat and allow to cool.

Melt the chocolate over a double boiler. Pour the cream into the melted chocolate and stir until fully incorporated. Remove from the heat and allow to cool to room temperature.

Using an electrical mixer, beat the butter until pale and doubled in volume. Gradually pour the melted chocolate mixture into the butter and stir until fully incorporated. Add the alcohol if using. Scrape down the sides of the bowl and refrigerate the chocolate ganache until firm.

Dip a Parisienne scoop into hot water, wipe dry and scoop ball-shaped truffles from the chocolate ganache. Roll the truffles in the cocoa powder.

Bring any remaining chocolate ganache back to room temperature and, using a palette knife, press it back together to form a block. Refrigerate until ready to be scooped out again to make more truffles. Chocolate truffles can be made in advance and stored in an airtight container.

Chocolate Soufflé

Serves 6

	softened butter for greasing soufflé dishes
60 g	castor sugar, plus extra for dusting soufflé dishes
175 g	dark chocolate (70% cocoa solids), chopped
4	large free-range eggs, separated
	drop of lemon juice
	icing sugar for dusting

Preheat the oven to 200 °C. Brush 6 ramekins (125 ml capacity) well with softened butter, using upwards strokes around the sides. Chill until firm, and then brush again with another layer of butter. Coat the ramekins with sugar, shaking out the excess. Place the ramekins on a baking tray and refrigerate until ready to use.

Put the chocolate into a stainless steel bowl and set over a pot of simmering water. Stir the chocolate until melted and smooth. Remove the bowl from the pot and allow to cool. Leave the pot of simmering water on the heat.

Measure the sugar into two 30 g amounts. Whisk the egg whites in a large bowl until they form firm peaks. Add a drop of lemon juice and whisk in 30 g of sugar, a tablespoon at a time, until the mixture forms stiff peaks.

Put the remaining 30 g of castor sugar and the egg yolks into a stainless steel bowl. Set over the pot of simmering water and whisk, making a sabayon until the eggs have tripled in volume. Remove from the pot and continue whisking until the sabayon cools down.

Fold the sabayon into the cooled chocolate, then fold in a spoonful of the egg whites to loosen the mixture. Carefully fold in the rest of the egg whites until fully incorporated into the chocolate. Spoon the mixture into the prepared ramekins and tap them lightly on the work surface to remove any air pockets. Bake for 8–10 minutes, until the soufflés are well risen and just set on the top but still moist in the centre. Dust with a little icing sugar and serve immediately.

White Chocolate and Passion Fruit Custard

Serves 8

60 g	castor sugar
7	free-range egg yolks
480 ml	fresh cream
½	pod vanilla, split lengthways and scraped
40 g	white chocolate, chopped
100 ml	passion fruit juice
	icing sugar for dusting

Preheat the oven to 100 °C.

Beat together 30 g of castor sugar and the egg yolks in a bowl until pale and doubled in volume and the sugar has dissolved.

In a heavy-based saucepan, add the remaining sugar, cream and vanilla and bring to the boil over medium heat.

Pour the hot cream into the egg yolks, mix well and then return to the saucepan. Cook very slowly over a gentle heat, stirring constantly until the mixture thickens enough to coat the back of a spoon. Remove from the heat, stir in the chocolate and passion fruit juice and mix until the chocolate has melted and is fully incorporated. Pass the custard through a fine sieve.

Pour the custard into desired moulds. Place the moulds into a roasting pan and pour hot water into the roasting pan to come three-quarters the way up the sides of the moulds. Cook the custard for 60–70 minutes, until they just reach setting point. Gently shake the tray. The custards will still be a little soft in the centre. If they appear to be too runny, return to the oven for a further 10 minutes. Carefully remove the roasting pan from the oven and allow the custards to cool down in the water bath. When cold, remove the custards from the water bath, cover with clingfilm and refrigerate for 8 hours, or preferably overnight.

To serve, dust each custard generously with icing sugar and glaze with a blowtorch until the sugar melts and begins to caramelise. Take care not to burn the sugar as it will become bitter. For a crisp glaze, dust and glaze the custard a second time.

Poached Pear, Chocolate Ganache and Pistachio

Serves 4

All of the different elements of this dessert can be made in advance and assembled at the last moment.

250 ml	**Chocolate Ganache (*page 259*)**
1 kg	**castor sugar**
1 ltr	**water**
4	**firm pears**
	juice of 1 lemon
50 g	**pistachio nuts, shelled and chopped**
40 ml	**Crème Anglaise (*Basic Recipe 55, page 232*)**

Make the chocolate ganache in advance and allow to set in the fridge.

Mix the sugar and water together in a heavy-based saucepan. Place over medium heat and stir until the sugar has dissolved. Bring to the boil, reduce the heat and continue to cook for 3 minutes. Pass through a fine sieve into a clean bowl and allow to cool. Store the sugar syrup in a sealed container in the fridge until ready to use.

Peel the pears using a swivel peeler, keeping the stalks attached. Rub the peeled pears with lemon juice to prevent them from discolouring. Pour the sugar syrup into a heavy-based saucepan and add the peeled pears. Cover with greaseproof paper and place a plate or smaller pot lid on top of the pears to keep them submerged in the syrup – if they are exposed to air they will discolour. Cook the pears over a very low heat for 10–12 minutes, until tender. Remove from the heat and allow the pears to cool in the syrup. Refrigerate until ready to use.

ASSEMBLING THE DESSERT

Remove the chocolate ganache from the fridge and allow to soften to a piping consistency. Remove the pears from the syrup and drain on kitchen paper. Cut the tops from the pears a third of the way down from the stalk and reserve. Hold the base of the pear in your hand and carefully scoop out the core. Hollow out the centre using a teaspoon or a Parisienne scoop, taking care not to break the pear wall. Place the chopped pistachio nuts in a shallow bowl and roll the pears in them until they have an even covering.

Spoon the chocolate ganache into a piping bag fitted with a 2 cm plain nozzle and fill the centre of each pear with the chocolate ganache. Place the pear in the centre of a bowl plate and top with the reserved pear 'lid'. Drizzle the crème anglaise around the pear and serve.

Apple Sorbet, Jelly and Calvados Sabayon

Makes 6 as a dessert or 18 as a pre-dessert

The different components of this dessert can all be made in advance. The jellies can be set and refrigerated. The sorbet can be churned and kept in the freezer until ready to serve. The sabayon can be refrigerated for 2 days – stir gently before serving so it is smooth. The dried apple can be made a day in advance and kept in an airtight container.

Apple Sorbet

Makes 550 ml approximately

300 ml	water
125 ml	clear apple juice
130 g	sugar
50 ml	liquid glucose
1	pod vanilla, split lengthways
300 g	Granny Smith apples, cored (unpeeled)
	juice of ½ lemon

Place the water, apple juice, sugar, glucose and vanilla in a heavy-based saucepan and bring to the boil. Reduce the heat and cook until the sugar and glucose have dissolved. Remove the syrup from the heat, pass through a fine chinois and allow to cool. When cold, add the apples to the syrup and blitz in a blender to a smooth purée; add lemon juice to taste. Pass through a fine chinois. Transfer to an ice-cream maker and churn until firm. Place in a container and freeze until ready to use.

Apple Jelly

Makes 650 ml approximately

420 ml	clear apple juice
165 ml	Sugar Syrup (*Basic Recipe 53, page 229*)
	leaves of gelatine, soaked in cold water and squeezed dry
35 ml	Calvados

Bring the apple juice and sugar syrup to the boil in a heavy-based saucepan. Add the gelatine and whisk until dissolved. Add the Calvados. Pour the jelly into glasses – one-third full – and allow to set for 3–4 hours in the fridge.

Calvados Sabayon

Makes 150 ml approximately

100 ml	Sugar Syrup (*Basic Recipe 53, page 229*)
1	free-range egg yolk
25 ml	Calvados
25 ml	fresh cream

Pour the sugar syrup, egg yolk and Calvados into a stainless steel bowl. Set over a pot of simmering water and whisk, making a sabayon until the eggs have tripled in volume. Remove from the pot and continue whisking until the sabayon cools down. Whip the cream to ribbon stage. Allow the sabayon to cool before folding the cream through it.

Dried Apple

1 **large, firm green apple without blemishes**
icing sugar

Preheat the oven to 85 °C. Slice the apple as thinly as possible. The best results are obtained by slicing on an electric slicing machine or a mandoline. Depending on the size of the apple, it should yield between 18 and 24 slices. Lay a silicone mat on a baking tray and cover it with a dusting of icing sugar. Arrange the sliced apple in rows on top of the icing sugar. Dust the exposed sides of the apple with icing sugar so that they are completely covered. Place in the oven and cook for 2 hours until they become golden and crisp. Gently remove the sliced apples with a palette knife and store in an airtight container until ready to use.

ASSEMBLING THE DESSERT

Spoon a layer of sorbet on top of the jelly so the glass is two-thirds full. Fill the remainder of the glass with the Calvados sabayon, garnish with a slice of dried apple and serve immediately.

Cherry Soup

Serves 4

Half of the cherries will be used to make the soup and the remaining cherries will be used for presentation. Select the choicest, unblemished cherries for presentation. The sugar syrup may be flavoured with cinnamon, star anise or mint. Cherry liqueur or a dash of Kirsch could be added to the soup or the whole cherries could be macerated in the alcohol until ready to serve to add a different flavour to the finished dish. Serve the soup chilled with a scoop of Vanilla Bean Ice Cream (*Basic Recipe 59, page 237*).

400 g	**dark cherries, pitted**
150 ml	**Sugar Syrup (*Basic Recipe 53, page 229*)**
½	**stick cinnamon**
1	**small sprig lemon thyme**
	icing sugar
1	**lemon**
12	**small fresh mint leaves**

Reserve half of the cherries for presentation and refrigerate until ready to serve. Bring the sugar syrup and cinnamon to the boil in a heavy-based saucepan over medium heat. Reduce the heat to a simmer and add the remaining cherries and lemon thyme. Cook the cherries for 5 minutes. Remove from the heat and allow the flavours to infuse for 1 hour.

Remove and discard the cinnamon stick and lemon thyme. Ladle the cherries and syrup into a liquidiser in batches and blend to a smooth purée. Taste the purée and add icing sugar and a squeeze of lemon juice if needed. Pass the soup through a fine sieve, pressing hard with the back of a ladle to extract as much flavour from the cherries as possible.

Pour the soup over the whole reserved cherries and refrigerate until ready to serve. To serve, divide the soup and cherries between four chilled bowl plates. Place a scoop of vanilla bean or cinnamon ice cream in the centre of the soup. Garnish with mint leaves and serve immediately.

Lemon Posset

Serves 4

This is a very simple yet impressive dessert. Serve simply with shortbread or with some Cherry Soup spooned over once set. Fresh strawberries or raspberries arranged on top and sprinkled with chopped green pistachios is also another simple garnish.

2	**lemons**
425 ml	**double cream**
125 g	**castor sugar**

Finely grate the zest from the lemons. Halve the lemons and squeeze out the juice. Strain the juice and measure out 115 ml.

Mix the cream, lemon zest and sugar in a heavy-based saucepan and bring to the boil, stirring occasionally until the sugar has dissolved. Reduce the heat and simmer for 3 minutes. Remove the pan from the heat and whisk in the lemon juice. Strain the cream into a jug, pressing the zest in the sieve to extract as much flavour as possible. Discard the zest.

Allow the mix to settle for 5 minutes before skimming the froth off the surface. Pour equal amounts of the lemon posset into glasses and leave to cool. Cover the glasses with clingfilm and refrigerate for 24 hours to set.

Iced Strawberry Soufflé

Serves 4

The soufflé can be made with other fruits, such as raspberries, peaches, plums or pineapples. You can also make one large soufflé; it will require longer freezing time. Don't freeze the soufflés for more than a few days as they will become too icy and lose their soft consistency.

750 g **strawberries**
365 ml **double cream**
1½ **free-range egg whites**
210 g **sugar**
juice of ½ lemon

Fold a sheet of greaseproof paper lengthways in three and tie it around the edge of a ramekin to form a collar, which should extend 5 cm above the rim of the ramekin. Repeat with the remaining 3 ramekins.

Rinse the strawberries under cold water, hull and reserve 150 g in the fridge. Purée the rest of the strawberries in a blender or food processor until smooth, then pass through a fine sieve to remove any seeds. Refrigerate until ready to use.

Whip the cream to ribbon stage and refrigerate until ready to use.

Beat the egg whites with 15 ml of the sugar until stiff peaks form.

Whisk the remaining sugar into the strawberry purée; add lemon juice to taste. Set 100 ml of the purée aside to use for garnishing the soufflé. Gently whisk the remaining purée into the cream until fully incorporated, taking care not to overbeat the cream. Fold the egg whites through the strawberry cream. Pour the mixture into the prepared ramekins and freeze for 8 hours until set.

Select 4 unblemished strawberries for garnishing the soufflés. Quarter the remaining strawberries and mix them into half of the reserved strawberry purée. Remove the greaseproof collars from the soufflé. Using a warm teaspoon, make a small well in the centre of each soufflé. Fill the cavity with the strawberry and purée mixture. Replace a little of the soufflé and smooth over the top with a palette knife. Place back in the freezer for 15 minutes to set.

To serve, place the soufflé onto a serving plate. Dip the reserved whole strawberries in the strawberry purée and place one on top of each soufflé. Serve the remaining purée separately in a sauceboat or jug.

Berry Consommé

Serves 4

This is not a classic consommé, as the berry juice is not clarified. However, once the berries are cooked, hung and passed the consommé becomes crystal clear and intensely flavoured. The berries must be slightly overripe for them to release all of their juices to receive maximum yield from them. With the addition of gelatine the consommé can be turned into a jelly to use as the base for other desserts. With the addition of water it can be turned into granita (*page 274*).

1 kg	**ripe strawberries**
200 g	**raspberries**
150 g	**castor sugar**
50 ml	**Champagne or sparkling wine (optional)**

Prepare the berry juice: Hull and roughly chop the strawberries. Place in a bowl with the raspberries and the castor sugar. Mix together and cover with clingfilm. Place the bowl over a pot of simmering water and leave for 1 hour over low heat. Remove from the heat and refrigerate for a further hour.

Line a sieve with a double layer of muslin cloth and place over a clean bowl. Pour the berry mix into the muslin cloth and allow the berry juice to filter through until only the dried berry pulp remains. Discard the pulp.

Serve the consommé with mixed berries and a selection of slice stone fruits, and a scoop of ice cream. Cut a selection of fruit, such as peaches and plums, in half, remove the stones and cut each half into 4 wedges. Cut figs into 6 wedges. Clean mixed berries if necessary and hull. Arrange the fruit in 4 chilled bowl plates. Stir the Champagne through the berry juice and pour over the fruit. Serve with a scoop of Vanilla Bean Ice Cream (*Basic Recipe 59, page 237*).

Strawberry Granita

Serves 4

Granita is simply a shaved ice made from a lightly sweetened fruit purée or other liquid such as coffee. Of all the frozen desserts, granita is the simplest to make, requiring nothing more than a dish, a freezer and a fork.

750 g **ripe strawberries**
50 g **castor sugar**

Hull the strawberries and reserve one-third for garnish. Chop the remainder and place them into a bowl with the sugar. Cover with clingfilm. Place the bowl over a pot of simmering water and leave for 1 hour over low heat until all the juice has been extracted from the strawberries. Allow to cool in the fridge for 1 hour before passing through a fine sieve. Discard the strawberry pulp.

Measure how much strawberry juice you have, save 100 ml and refrigerate until ready to serve. Stir 100 ml water into the remaining strawberry juice, pour it into a shallow tray and freeze for 3–4 hours until partially frozen. Take the semi-frozen granita from the freezer and, using a fork, stir the frozen crystals into the liquid. Return to the freezer. Repeat this process twice more during freezing to achieve a granular texture.

Divide the reserved strawberries between 4 chilled glasses, pour over 25 ml of the reserved strawberry juice, and scrape shavings off the frozen block of granita with a fork. Spoon the granita on top, filling the glass to two-thirds full. Serve immediately.

BASIC KNIFE SKILLS

Whether slicing cheese, peeling asparagus, jointing a chicken or filleting a fish, there is a knife designed for each task. Your personal knives should be tailored to suit your needs as a cook.

As with any job, a task is easier to complete effectively and effortlessly if you are using the appropriate tool. Food preparation is no different. A boning knife, for example, is specifically designed to separate meat from the bone easily, and its shape and blade is suited to manoeuvre around bones. Using another type of knife, such as a cook's knife or paring knife, will not only prove difficult, but simply won't be as effective.

When buying knives, buy the best quality that you can afford, and instead of buying a large set of knives, start by investing in a few quality ones and add to the collection over time as needed. If bought well and looked after, each knife should last a lifetime.

A good knife should feel well balanced and sturdy in your hand. It should have a comfortable handle and a deep forged shoulder or finger guard.

Slotted or magnetic knife blocks are the safest way to store knives, although these can be bulky and take up a lot of work space. Magnetic knife strips mounted to the wall are also a great way of keeping knives safe and easily visible and accessible during cooking. Avoid storing knives in drawers unless you have a proper knife system. The blades are easily damaged if knives are left loose in a drawer.

In the event that you need to transport your knives, knife rolls and cases are the best way to store them safely during transport. Keep knife rolls in a good condition as holes may appear over time and the knives may protrude or slip through, causing injury.

Sharpen your knives regularly. A blunt knife will not make a sharp or clean cut and the added work and pressure involved in trying to make such a knife perform can be dangerous, as well as frustrating and time consuming. A blunt knife is much more likely to slip and cause injury than a sharp knife, and will result in a much worse cut than that received from a sharp knife.

It is very important to always keep both the handle and blade of your knife clean when using it, especially when preparing fatty foods. A wet or greasy blade may cause the knife to slip when cutting. Most knives are dishwasher proof, but the long cycle and heat of the dishwasher can affect the tempering, so this manner of cleaning should be avoided. Hand wash knives separately with detergent and warm water before drying with a clean tea towel.

OTHER POINTS TO CONSIDER

- Never leave knives in a sink, especially if it is full of hot soapy water. Apart from having a detrimental effect on both the blade and handle of a knife, it is all too easy to reach into a sink full of soapy water and inadvertently grab a knife by the blade.
- Always walk with the knife down by your side.
- Never attempt to catch a falling knife.
- Keep your knives in good condition; sharpen either before or after every use, as automatically as you would wash them.
- Keep ingredients as cold as possible, particularly meat, poultry and fish. This is not only more hygienic, but also ensures ingredients are as firm as possible, making them easier to cut.
- Put a damp cloth underneath your chopping board to steady it when working.
- Work in a tidy and organised manner. Finish one task and clean your work surface before starting another.
- Avoid using a knife if your hands are wet or greasy. You need to maintain a steady grip on the knife's handle if you are to remain in complete control.
- Be confident, but always alert – you are using a sharp implement.

BLOCKING OFF

The process of removing the curved edges from an ingredient so that the remaining shape is regular, from which uniform shapes can then be cut.

BRUNOISE

Vegetables, fruit, meat and so forth cut into very small, even-sized dice.

BUTTERFLYING

The process of removing the bone or shell from an ingredient and opening it out like a 'butterfly'. The process is often applied to a spatchcock or prawns.

CARPACCIO

An Italian term originally for thinly sliced, raw beef or fish, although the term is now loosely applied to describe any thinly sliced raw ingredient.

Chopping

Dicing

Julienne

Lardons

Parisienne

Peeling

Segmenting

Slicing

Using a Mandoline

CHIFFONADE
Describes herbs or leafy green vegetables (such as basil and spinach) cut into long, thin strips. This is accomplished by stacking and rolling leaves, then cutting across the rolled leaves with a sharp knife, producing fine ribbons.

CHINED
A cut of meat that contains the bones that connect the ribs to the backbone, or the backbone itself (chine bone).

CHOPPING
The most common cutting method. The knife tip is used as a support and constantly moves, but maintains contact with the board throughout. The whole length of the knife is brought backwards and then is moved forwards in a rolling motion. The ingredient gets the full benefit of the knife's blade.

CONCASSÉE
A term to describe a uniform dice of blanched, peeled and seeded tomatoes (*Basic Technique 13, page 177*).

DICING
To cut into small, even-shaped cubes using a chopping knife.

ESCALOPE
A thin slice of meat or fish.

FILLETING
The process of removing the fillets from a piece of fish (*Basic Technique 6, page 111*) or meat using a filleting knife.

JULIENNE
Describes vegetables that have been cut into very fine strips, the length of a matchstick, using a chopping knife.

LARDON
A thin strip of salt pork, bacon or pancetta that is normally briefly blanched to remove any excess salt and then sautéed and served in salads, casseroles or as a garnish with braised meats. Lardons are sometimes inserted into lean cuts of meat to keep them moist and to add flavour during cooking.

PARING
To cut away the outer leaves or inedible parts of fruit and vegetables using a paring knife.

PIN BONING
The method of removing small bones from fish, usually using fish tweezers.

SCORING
The process of making a shallow incision. Scoring the skin on a duck or pork belly aids the rendering of the fat beneath the skin's surface.

SHUCKING
To open an oyster with an oyster knife (*Basic Technique 4, page 100*).

SNIPPING

To cut herbs finely with scissors to avoid bruising delicate herbs such as basil.

TUNNEL BONING

The process of removing a bone without opening up the meat *(page 156)* using a boning knife.

TURNING

To cut vegetables such as carrots, cucumbers and potatoes into small, even barrel shapes using a specially designed turning knife.

INDEX

Page numbers in **bold** indicate photographs.

F

G

H

I

J

K

L

M

N

O

T

V

W

The Author

Liam Tomlin was born in Dublin, Ireland, where his career as a chef began at the age of 14. He went on to gain experience in some of Ireland's and Europe's finest kitchens, eventually moving to Australia in 1991. For the next six years Liam worked with Dietmar Sawyer of Restaurant Forty One as Chef de Cuisine, honing his skills and accumulating invaluable knowledge from one of the world's finest chefs.

In 1997, Liam opened Banc Restaurant in Sydney, Australia, where his commitment to exceptional standards in service and cuisine garnered Banc many accolades.

Liam has worked alongside culinary icons Michel Roux (Snr), Shaun Hill, Richard Corrigan, Mark Edwards and renowned Master of Wine, Jancis Robinson. In 2001 he reached the finals of the inaugural World Master of Culinary Arts award honouring the world's leading chefs.

Liam and his wife, Jan, moved to Cape Town in 2004, where he established his consultancy company, *Beyond Food*. Liam's latest venture, *Chefs Warehouse & Cookery School*, is located in the heart of Cape Town and in the food capital, Franschhoek. It offers a combination of retail and culinary education: The *Warehouse* retails quality equipment, unique food products and cookbooks to both trade and public, while the *School* is a natural extension of Liam's passion for fine cuisine and his enthusiasm for training young chefs to the highest standards.

Liam is the author of *BANC* and *Season to Taste*.

The Photographer

Russell Smith is a passionate professional photographer, inspired by the city that surrounds him. A born Capetonian, he trained as an art director both here and in Paris, before turning his eye to photography.

Russell works with either natural light or with flash, but is always exacting about the details of a shoot. His work has focused on food, lifestyle, travel and portraiture, with food photography a big part of his portfolio. He has shot food photographs for a range of South African magazines as well as for top hotels and restaurants.

Russell frequently shoots on location internationally – from Tuscany to Istanbul, and from Mauritius to Botswana.